MATTHEW ARNOLD

By G. F. WATTS (*National Portrait Gallery*)

ARNOLD

Poetry & Prose

With

WILLIAM WATSON'S POEM

and Essays by

LIONEL JOHNSON & H. W. GARROD

With an Introduction and Notes by

E. K. CHAMBERS

OXFORD

AT THE CLARENDON PRESS

Oxford University Press, Amen House, London E.C.4

GLASGOW NEW YORK TORONTO MELBOURNE WELLINGTON
BOMBAY CALCUTTA MADRAS CAPE TOWN

Geoffrey Cumberlege, Publisher to the University

FIRST EDITION 1939
REPRINTED 1942, 1946, 1948, 1950

PRINTED IN GREAT BRITAIN

CONTENTS

INTRODUCTION

MATTHEW ARNOLD'S verse belongs mainly to his days of Oxford and youthful travel, and although the creative impulse occasionally revisited him thereafter, it was only in the interspaces of a long critical activity, devoted to the exploration of the fundamental elements of civilization, of the bearing of these on English politics and religion, and of literature as itself primarily 'a criticism of life'. Some of the earliest poems are related to a broken love-affair, with one of whom we know little more than that her name was Marguerite, that she was a blue-eyed 'daughter of France', and that Arnold met her at Thun in Switzerland.

The first love of a poet can never be without interest, or without significance. But we need not inquire too closely how much in the lyrics evoked by Marguerite is a literal transcript from experience, and how much grew up round that experience when it was in fact over. These are delicate things to handle.

> Tread softly because you tread on my dreams.

Certainly the parting with a blue-eyed girl became for Matthew Arnold something more than itself, a parting with a whole world of passionate romance which he put behind him. The Marguerite poems are not merely poems of isolation, but of renunciation, of self-dedication. There had been a κάθαρσις. He turned back to his 'spherèd course', to the rigorous teachers who had seized his youth, to

> The dragon-warder'd fountains
> Where the springs of knowledge are,

and incidentally to the routine, which he often found irksome, of a civil servant. But these early poems have a lyric plangency, which is not quite the note of those that followed.

Poetry, indeed, he did not lay aside, but for a time it took a more impersonal form, on classical models which were always dear to him. By 1853 he was at work upon *Sohrab and Rustum*, which appeared later in the year with the famous preface, in which Arnold laid down that 'the eternal objects of Poetry, among all nations, and at all times' are 'actions; human actions; possessing an inherent interest in themselves, and which are to be communicated in an interesting manner by the art of the Poet'. This was consonant enough with his own mood when it was written. But it is a curious limitation of the scope of high poetry, the criterion of which, on the side of impulse, as distinct from craftsmanship, is surely to be found, not in the nature of its subject matter, but in the quality of the emotional excitement which that subject matter, whether a human action or some simple fact of observation, or feeling, or reflection, has aroused in the mind of the poet. Matthew Arnold has said many sound things about poets and poems, and in particular about poetic diction, but I do not think that he was ever at his best in attempting to expound the fundamental basis of poetic activity. He comes nearer to the truth in a much later essay, at the point where, after exalting Wordsworth over other poets because he deals with more of life, and deals with it, as a whole, more powerfully than they do, he is suddenly taken aback at finding himself in apparent agreement with the logical but eminently prosaic mind of Leslie Stephen. Wordsworth's poetry was great, according to Leslie Stephen, because his philosophy was sound. 'No', says Arnold, 'Wordsworth's poetry is great because of the extraordinary power with which Wordsworth feels the joy offered to us in nature, the joy offered to us in the simple primary affections and duties; and because of the extraordinary power with which, in case after case, he shows us this joy, and renders it so as to make us share it.' But I will not here consider Matthew Arnold as a critic. He wrote *Sohrab and Rustum*, with 'more pleasure than anything I have done yet'. And it is a noble poem, the fruit of his constant preoccupation with Homer, whose works, he says, for one or two years, were seldom out of his hands. But it is no mere transcript from Homer. It is Homeric in its large utterance, its forthrightness, its constant use of expanded similes; un-Homeric and modern in its concentration on a theme of family relationship such as Homer only lightly touches, in the more conscious elaboration of its decorative passages, and above all in the enveloping presence of the river Oxus, which is a recurrent note throughout, and culminates in the magnificent *finale*, too familiar for me to quote, where the father and the son are left alone on the darkling plain, and the Oxus, regardless and serene, moves onward to the Aral sea.

During the next decade, Arnold's poems came slowly, although, as gathered in the volume of 1867, they form a substantial body, of unimpaired poetic quality. They close, indeed, with the *Thyrsis* of 1866, which is perhaps his finest single work. But educational duties pressed upon him throughout, and in 1857 the Professorship of Poetry turned his thoughts to prose. Probably his poetic impulse never flowed easily. Over *Thyrsis* itself he brooded long. Clough, on whom it was in part written, died in 1861. Arnold had meant to begin it at Oxford in the spring of 1863, but was prevented by 'a detestable cold wind'. He could do no more, he wrote, than accumulate stores for it. In the same letter he notes the fritillaries in the meadows by the Thames. All the images in *Thyrsis*, he said later, were from actual observation. The cuckoo, however, was heard, not at Hinksey, but at Woodford, in Epping Forest, during 1864. The poem, therefore, took at least two or three years in the making. There is much evidence that at all times in this decade Arnold found the writing of poetry difficult. Another letter, of 1858, is in the nature of an *apologia* for *Merope*. It was motived by the temptation 'if you cannot bear anything not *very good*, to transfer your operations to a region where form is everything'. A kind of perfection might thus be approached. But to attain perfection in thought and feeling, as well as in form, seemed to him impossible, 'unless one can devote one's whole life to poetry', as Wordsworth, Shelley, Byron, and Tennyson were able to do. Probably Matthew Arnold was carrying too great a load of competing activities. But I do not myself believe in the doctrine of a complete dedication to poetry. Poetry is, after all, the reflex of life, and life, if its reflex is to be of value, must be lived for itself. It is remarkable how much of the world's greatest poetry has in fact been written by men who largely spent themselves in normal occupations, and, on the other hand, how dilute the poetry of live-long poets has often become. Wordsworth is an outstanding example of this. It is no part of my object to attempt a comparison between the best work of Matthew Arnold and that of his greatest contemporaries. Personal taste and emotional sympathy inevitably play too great a part in any such estimate. But one may fairly maintain that the *proportion* of work which endures is greater in the case of Matthew Arnold than in that of any one of them. Nevertheless it is true that in middle life he came more and more to feel poetry slipping away from him, and that for this his preoccupations were at least in part responsible. More than once he resolved to lay critical writings aside and return to the Muses. 'The period between forty and fifty', he wrote in 1861, 'is not a bad ten years of one's life for poetry, if one resolutely uses it, but it is a time in which, if one does not use it, one dries up and becomes prosaic.' One does, no doubt. But his hopes were not to be realized. Forty saw him plunged in educational controversy, and on the eve of those long inquiries into the conditions of foreign schools, which were destined to have so profound an ultimate influence upon the development of education in this country. And these in their turn were followed by the remarkable

essays on the trend of English civilization, social and religious, which have done more than we always realize to
determine our modern apprehension of spiritual values.
Matthew Arnold's poetic activity practically closed with
the volume of 1867. Even so, twenty years was a reasonable
span. As it happens, it was just that of Shakespeare's
poetic life, and of Spenser's. The Destinies gave Shelley no
more than twelve, and Keats no more than five. Wordsworth's poetic life, rightly measured, was about ten.
Perhaps Arnold recognized the inevitable, when he issued
his collection of 1869. It was not quite complete. One of
the omitted poems was *The Voice*, in which he detected a
tone of falsetto. I do not myself feel that there is much
falsetto, if by that is meant the kind of thing which you get
in *Maud* and *Locksley Hall*, and some other of the less
successful attempts of Tennyson. But Arnold was always
fastidious. One or two other poems were more or less re-
written. The texts of the rest do not differ substantially
from the earlier ones. But there was a good deal of touching
up, generally for the better, in small details of craftsmanship. Clashes of sound and repetition of epithets were
eliminated. Arnold, like meaner men, was occasionally
worried by the difficulty of securing the right alternation of
'that' and 'which'. And there are some amusing alterations
due to the increased knowledge of field botany which he
acquired in his later years. The original blue convolvulus
on the stubble field of *The Gipsy Scholar* becomes a pink one.
The reaping scene of *Bacchanalia* is turned into a mowing
scene, because the dog-rose is over before harvest time. The
'green fern' of *Tristram and Iseult* gives place to 'last
year's fern', because that is what you really get in April.
Another example of Arnold's desire for literal fidelity of
visual rendering is also to be found in *The Scholar Gipsy*.
Instead of 'the slow punt swings round' he put 'the punt's
rope chops round'. It is less elegant, but the punt at

Bablock-hythe is so fixed as to make a moving bridge which
cannot swing round. Arnold lived for nearly twenty years
after the collection of 1869 was issued. Even to the end he
was still occasionally wondering, rather wistfully, whether
he should ever do anything more in poetry. 'It is something', he adds, 'to have been of use in prose.' And so,
indeed, it is. The occasional pieces, mostly elegies on house-
hold pets, of these later years, although gracefully turned,
do not amount to much.

I turn to another aspect of Matthew Arnold's poetry. The
elegiac temper pervades it from beginning to end, and it is
perhaps this, rather than the exaltation of the early lyric,
or the deep harmony of *Sohrab and Rustum*, which seems to
the modern reader his peculiar characteristic. The elegy,
as is common with elegy, often has an idyllic setting. For
such writing as that of *The Scholar Gipsy* and *Thyrsis*, and
of some passages in *Resignation* and *Bacchanalia*, I will
venture to borrow the phrase of a poetess who herself
wrote no poetry, 'It calls home the heart to quietness'.
The country dear to Matthew Arnold was very quiet
country. Hinksey and Cumnor, the haunts of his youth and
mine, to which he always returned on his visits to Oxford,
were not what are called beauty spots. They were merely
uplands of ancient pasture, down some of which, by the
time of *Thyrsis*, the ploughboy's team had already gone;
with a bit of woodland, a wide outlook over Oxford itself
and the surrounding valleys, and little footpaths running
from farm to farm beneath high hedges. You may taste
such quietness in any part of England still, if you care to
leave the roadways. Arnold has other scenery as well; that
of the Lake Country, that of a Surrey common, with its
hollies, in *Tristram and Iseult*, that of the lower Alps, where
the yellow gentian flames on the way to

> Jaman, delicately tall,
> Above his sun-warm'd firs;

that of Sicily in *Empedocles on Etna*, with its classical
reminiscences. It is all quiet. From all alike he draws the
cool refreshment of which I have already spoken. You will
find, if you run through the poems, that 'cool' is his
favourite epithet. And above all he loves the coolest things
in the world, the dew at morning and in the evening, and
the moon. How many of his best things are drenched in
moonlight. The Merman creeps to shore,

> When clear falls the moonlight,
> When spring-tides are low.

In *The Youth of Nature*,

> The lake,
> Lovely and soft as a dream,
> Swims in the sheen of the moon.

The Scholar Gipsy has its 'moon-blanched green', *Dover
Beach* its 'moon-blanch'd land', *A Summer Night* its
'moon-blanch'd street'; and both this and *A Southern
Night* recall an unforgotten experience in which the moon
had its part. The moon, again, shines on Tristram's death-
bed, and through the clerestory windows of *The Church at
Brou*. The Oxus flows through the hushed Chorasmian
waste 'under the solitary moon'. Apollo and the Muses in
Empedocles roam through the 'moon-silver'd inlets' of
Thisbe vale. The nightingale of *Philomela* sings in the
moonlit cedar. The full moon lights the 'groups under the
dreaming garden-trees' in *Thyrsis*. The quietness of Arnold's
vision is enhanced by the quality of his verse; its simplicity,
lucidity, and straightforwardness; its literalness, I think he
would have said; the sparing use of aureate words, or of
far-fetched words, which are all the more effective when they
come; the avoidance of inversions, and the general direct-
ness of syntax, which gives full value to the delicacies of a
varied rhythm, and makes it, of all verse that I know, the
easiest to read aloud. Here are some at least of the characteristics which Arnold found in Homer and did not find in

some of Homer's translators. But it was only in *Sohrab and Rustum* and *Balder* that he essayed the Homeric grandeur. The diction of *Thyrsis* he says, was modelled on that of Theocritus. He felt that it was 'a very quiet poem'.

As a poet of natural beauty Matthew Arnold is the direct inheritor of Wordsworth. He acknowledges the derivation more than once; in *The Youth of Nature* and in the *Memorial Verses*. And like Wordsworth, the Wordsworth of 'The world is too much with us', he contrasts the quiet of nature with the disquietude of man,

> This iron time
> Of doubts, disputes, distractions, fears,

the 'benumbing round', the 'faded, ignoble lives' of world-lings, the

> Strange disease of modern life,
> With its sick hurry, its divided aims.

He looks upon

> The long heart-wasting show,
> Wherein earth's great ones are disquieted.

Man is 'the eternal trifler':

> We see all sights from pole to pole,
> And glance, and nod, and bustle by,
> And never once possess our soul
> Before we die.

The thought is more habitual than in Wordsworth. And indeed the parallel between Wordsworth and Arnold must not be pushed too far. They differed both in temper and in conviction. We have seen that what Arnold felt most clearly in Wordsworth's reaction to nature and life was joy. But the poet of *Resignation*, written around those fells of Watendlath which Wordsworth knew so well, has another outlook. He too, as he leans on his gate in the misty morn-ing, sees the whole of life unroll before him, just as Words-worth might have done. But for him it is a life

> Whose secret is not joy, but peace.

And again:

> Yet, Fausta, the mute turf we tread,
> The solemn hills around us spread,
> This stream which falls incessantly,
> The strange-scrawled rocks, the lonely sky,
> If I might lend their life a voice,
> Seem to bear rather than rejoice.

Nor were the spiritual implications in Wordsworth's matured poetry of nature such as Arnold could accept. Content as a boy to take 'the harvest of a quiet eye', or at the most aware in retrospect of dim intimations pointing to unknown modes of being, Wordsworth found his way to a conviction, based on mystic intuition rather than logical reasoning, of a universal harmony in things. The life of man is bound up with the life of nature, and together they are the vehicle of a power that informs them both. This doctrine finds its clearest expression in the lines on *Tintern Abbey*, although ultimately Wordsworth gave it a more specifically Christian turn.

> I have felt
> A presence that disturbs me with the joy
> Of elevated thoughts: a sense sublime
> Of something far more deeply interfused,
> Whose dwelling is the light of setting suns,
> And the round ocean, and the living air,
> And the blue sky, and in the mind of man:
> A motion and a spirit, that impels
> All thinking things, all objects of all thought,
> And rolls through all things.

This philosophic optimism, if the term is not too intellectual a one to use, was never Matthew Arnold's. His rigorous teachers had purged his faith, and shown him 'the high, white star of Truth', and in that clear and searching light he could see no certainty of such a harmony. His prevailing elegiac mood is one of disequilibrium. He can arrive at no coherent vision of the scheme of things entire. Nature

follows the course of nature, and man follows the course of
man. Between these there may be contacts. Man may learn
endurance as well as peace from nature, when

> With joy the stars perform their shining,
> And the sea its long moon-silver'd roll.

It is the lesson of the sonnet on *Toil and Tranquillity*, which
once stood at the head of his first volume. The 'sleepless
ministers' of nature are the 'labourers that shall not fail,
when man is gone'. But what assurance is there that even
the reasonable strivings of men serve a divine end? We
strive to little purpose:

> Unbreachable the fort
> Of the long-battered world uplifts its wall.

And we strive blindly:

> We are here as on a darkling plain
> Swept with confused alarms of struggle and flight,
> Where ignorant armies clash by night.

Once again the sense of isolation is strong upon him. At
the best we are 'in some unknown Power's employ'. Arnold
stood too near his lost faith to become a contented pagan.
He feels as one adrift from his moorings. He envies the
Scholar Gipsy, in his single-eyed chase, year after year, of
a constant aim,

> Still nursing the unconquerable hope,
> Still clutching the inviolable shade.

He envies the calm security of the Carthusian in his cell,
regardless of the banners and the bugles of the outer
world:

> Like these, on earth I wait forlorn.
> Their faith, my tears, the world deride—
> I come to shed them at their side.

But the 'cloister-floor of humid stone' is not for him; and
indeed he would have been ill at ease on it.

It is possible to lay too much emphasis upon this side of

Arnold's poetry. That is an error of perspective into which, I think, some of his critics have fallen. After all, the elegies only represent one factor in a complex personality, reacting from strenuous days of unfaltering devotion to the service of what is best in humanity. Arnold was no Obermann, sadly watching the irretrievable flux of things from the door of his high chalet on the green slopes of Jaman. The pulse of living in him was too strong for that stern withdrawal and its 'hourly varied anodynes'. To that 'unstrung will' and 'broken heart' he bade farewell, with much else, when he returned to his 'spherèd course'. A visit to Glion brought an hour of recollection:

> An eremite with thee, in thought
> Once more I slip my chain.

But although Obermann had been 'the master of my wandering youth', he had then been 'left for many a year'. One must not expect to find consistency in the moods of a poet. Often enough, natural beauty seems to be for Arnold a mere *refrigerium*. But it is not always so. There is at least meliorism, if not optimism, at the end of *Obermann Once More*, as the dawn breaks over the Valais; and again in *The Future*, where the river of Time, in 'wider, statelier' flow, may yet strike peace to the soul of humanity,

> As the stars come out, and the night-wind
> Brings up the stream
> Murmurs and scents of the infinite sea.

Nor is the tonic strain of 'unresting, unhasting' endeavour a rare one. It is something more than mere acceptance; rather the spirit of morality suffused by emotion which Arnold found in Marcus Aurelius, 'a spirit not so much of gladness and elation, as of gentleness and sweetness; a delicate and tender sentiment, which is less than joy and more than resignation'. It informs, very notably, the musings over the example of Arnold's own father in *Rugby*

Chapel. The testament of Empedocles to Pausanias does not show the poet's thought at its clearest, or give it its finest expression, but here too is such consolation as a stoic may take. Life has a bounty for man, if he will only be moderate in his demands on it:

> Is it so small a thing
> To have enjoy'd the sun,
> To have lived light in the spring,
> To have loved, to have thought, to have done;
> To have advanced true friends, and beat down baffling foes?
>
> I say: Fear not! Life still
> Leaves human effort scope.
> But, since life teems with ill,
> Nurse no extravagant hope:
> Because thou must not dream, thou needs't not then despair.

ACKNOWLEDGEMENTS

Thanks are due to the British Academy for their consent to the adaptation of the Editor's Warton Lecture on Matthew Arnold as an Introduction; to Lady Watson and Messrs. Harrap and Co. for the use of Sir William Watson's poem; to Mr. Elkin Mathews for that of a passage from Lionel Johnson's *Post Liminium*; to Professor Garrod and the Harvard University Press for that of passages from *Poetry and the Criticism of Life*; to the National Portrait Gallery for permission to reproduce the portrait by G. F. Watts; to Professor D. Nichol Smith for valuable suggestions; and to Professor J. Boyd for help in tracing some of Arnold's references to Goethe.

ARNOLD'S LIFE

1822. Born at Laleham, Surrey (Dec. 24), son of Rev. Thomas Arnold and Mary Penrose.
1828. Father becomes Headmaster of Rugby.
1830. Pupil of uncle, Rev. John Buckland, at Laleham.
1832. Father buys Fox How, Ambleside.
1836. Sent to Winchester College.
1837. Removed to Rugby School.
1840. School prize for poem *Alaric at Rome* (printed).
1841. Open scholarship at Balliol College, Oxford.
1842. Father dies (June 12).
1843. Newdigate prize for poem on *Cromwell* (printed), but Commemoration too uproarious for recitation.
1844. Second Class in Literae Humaniores (Nov.).
1845. Teaches at Rugby. Fellowship at Oriel College, Oxford (March 28).
1846. France (Aug.).
1847. Private secretary to Marquis of Lansdowne, President of the Council.
1848. Switzerland (Sept.).
1849. *The Strayed Reveller, and Other Poems* (Feb.), soon withdrawn. Switzerland (Sept.).
1850. Death of Wordsworth (Apr. 23).
1851. Inspector of Schools (Apr. 14). Marries Frances Lucy Wightman (June 10).
1852. *Empedocles on Etna, and Other Poems* (Oct.).
1853. *Poems. A New Edition* (reprints, 1854, 1857).
1854. Belgium (July).
1855. *Poems. Second Series.*
1856. Elected to Athenaeum (Feb. 17).
1857. Professor of Poetry at Oxford (May 5). Inaugural Lecture on *The Modern Element in Literature.* Probably Switzerland (July).
1858. Takes 2 Chester Square, London (Feb.). Switzerland (July–Sept.). *Merope.*
1859. Foreign Assistant Commissioner to Education Commission. France, Holland, Switzerland (Apr.–Aug.). *England and the Italian Question* (July).
1860. Belgium (Sept., Oct.). *The Popular Education of France.*
1861. Clough dies (Nov. 13). *On Translating Homer.*
1862. Criticizes Lowe's Education Code. Belgium (Aug.). *Last Words on Translating Homer.*

1863. *The Bishop and the Philosopher* (on Colenso).

1864. *A French Eton.*

1865. France, Italy, Germany, Switzerland (Apr.–Nov.) for Schools Enquiry Commission. *Essays in Criticism* (1st Series, revised 1869, 1874).

1866. *Thyrsis* (Apr.). *Report on Secondary Education in Foreign Countries* (May).

1867. Professorship ends. *The Study of Celtic Literature. New Poems.*

1868. Moves to Harrow (Mar.). Deaths of sons Basil and Thomas.

1869. *Poems* in collected edition, with revised text. Later editions, with alterations (1877, 1881, 1885, 1890). *Culture and Anarchy.*

1870. D.C.L., Oxford. *St. Paul and Protestantism.*

1871. France, Switzerland (Aug.). *Friendship's Garland.*

1872. *A Bible Reading for Schools: The Great Prophecy of Israel's Restoration.*

1873. Moves to Pain's Hill Cottage, Cobham, Surrey (June). *Literature and Dogma.*

1875. *God and the Bible.*

1877. *Last Essays on Church and Religion.*

1878. France (Sept., Oct.). *Select Poems* (Golden Treasury).

1879. *Mixed Essays.*

1880. Italy, Switzerland (Sept.). *Prose Passages.* Contributions to Ward's *English Poets.*

1881. Burke's *Letters, Speeches, and Tracts on Irish Affairs* (edited).

1882. *Irish Essays.*

1883. Civil List Pension of £250 (Aug.). America (Oct. to Mar. 1884). *Isaiah of Jerusalem.*

1885. Declines re-nomination for Oxford Professorship. France, Switzerland, Germany (Nov., Dec.) for Royal Commission on Education. *Discourses in America.*

1886. France, Switzerland, Germany (Feb., Mar.). Resigns Inspectorship (Apr. 30). America (May–Aug.). *Report on Certain Points Connected with Elementary Education in Germany, Switzerland, and France.*

1888. Dies (Apr. 15). Burial at Laleham. *Essays in Criticism. Second Series* (posthumous).

1889. *Reports on Elementary Schools* (1852–82), ed. Sir Francis Sandford.

WILLIAM WATSON

In Laleham Churchyard

From *Poems* (1892)

'TWAS at this season, year by year,
The singer who lies songless here
Was wont to woo a less austere,
 Less deep repose,
Where Rotha to Winandermere
 Unresting flows,—

Flows through a land where torrents call
To far-off torrents as they fall,
And mountains in their cloudy pall
 Keep ghostly state,
And Nature makes majestical
 Man's lowliest fate.

There, 'mid the August glow, still came
He of the twice-illustrious name,
The loud impertinence of fame
 Not loth to flee—
Not loth with brooks and fells to claim
 Fraternity.

Linked with his happy youthful lot,
Is Loughrigg, then, at last forgot?
Nor silent peak nor dalesman's cot
 Looks on his grave.
Lulled by the Thames he sleeps, and not
 By Rotha's wave.

'Tis fittest thus! for though with skill
He sang of beck and tarn and ghyll,
The deep, authentic mountain-thrill
 Ne'er shook his page!
Somewhat of worldling mingled still
 With bard and sage.

And 'twere less meet for him to lie
Guarded by summits lone and high
That traffic with the eternal sky
 And hear, unawed,
The everlasting fingers ply
 The loom of God,

Than, in this hamlet of the plain,
A less sublime repose to gain,
Where Nature, genial and urbane,
 To man defers,
Yielding to us the right to reign,
 Which yet is hers.

And nigh to where his bones abide,
The Thames with its unruffled tide
Seems like his genius typified,—
 Its strength, its grace,
Its lucid gleam, its sober pride,
 Its tranquil pace.

But ah! not his the eventual fate
Which doth the journeying wave await—
Doomed to resign its limpid state
 And quickly grow
Turbid as passion, dark as hate,
 And wide as woe.

Rather, it may be, over-much
He shunned the common stain and smutch,
From soilure of ignoble touch
 Too grandly free,
Too loftily secure in such
 Cold purity.

But he preserved from chance control
The fortress of his 'stablisht soul;
In all things sought to see the Whole;
 Brooked no disguise;
And set his heart upon the goal,
 Not on the prize;

And with those few he shall survive
Who seem not to compete or strive,
Yet with the foremost still arrive,
 Prevailing still:
The Elect with whom the stars connive
 To work their will.

LIONEL JOHNSON

From *Post Liminium* (1911)

THE more complete poems of Matthew Arnold are little more than one hundred in number. Of these, only five are of considerable length. So careful and discreet an achievement, during some forty years, ought to come close upon perfection: and this it does. But of Arnold's rare and happy qualities we will speak later; let us first have done with his few and venial faults. There are lines, phrases, and constructions, not perfectly polished; and there are poems, or stanzas, not perfectly poetical. That is, there are faults of expression and of conception. Arnold, as Lord Coleridge tells us, had a most imperfect ear for music. Now, while no one questions his wonderful ear for the cadence of verse, it is equally true that his sense for melody sometimes failed him. Within one short poem occur two such discordant lines as 'There the pines slope, the cloud strips', and 'Where the high woods strip sadly'. It explains Arnold's avowed preference for the rhythm of

> Siehst sehr sterbeblässlich aus,

over the rhythm of

> Que dit le ciel à l'aube, et la flamme à la flamme ?

Again, the construction is at times forced, as in

> That furtive mien, that scowling eye,
> Of hair that red and tufted fell—

where the second line 'is only poetry because it is not prose'. These technical faults are few, and they are less troublesome than the foolish affectations of much modern workmanship. The second fault, faults of conception, is more serious. Arnold rarely fails to write in a spirit of singular loftiness and beauty; he is rarely neglectful of his own precept:

> Such, poets, is your bride, the Muse! young, gay,
> Radiant, adorn'd outside; a hidden ground
> Of thought and of austerity within.

But, at times, the thought is unadorned and the austerity far from radiant. To take an example:

> 'Religious fervours! ardour misapplied!
>   Hence, hence,' they cry, 'ye do but keep man blind!
> But keep him self-immersed, preoccupied,
>   And lame the active mind!'

Contrast that, in its nakedness, with the ornament and the radiance of the preceding poem: a poem full, too, of austere thought:

> So, in its lovely moonlight, lives the soul,
>   Mountains surround it, and sweet virgin air;
> Cold plashing, past it, crystal waters roll:
>   We visit it by moments, ah, too rare!

At once we feel that the first lines are not interesting, not heightened, not touched with emotion; that the second are no less beautiful than elevated.

These things are worth a few words, because the admirers of Arnold are in danger of being held his worshippers also, unless they show themselves aware of his faults. Arnold, great and admirable as he is, is no more perfect than is Gray, Milton, or Sophocles; but he stands above the first, and the others were his most successful masters.

Arnold's poems are of two kinds: there are the narrative poems, whether dramatic or otherwise; and the lyrical, emotional, or meditative poems. Now, it is observable that Arnold is at his best in poems neither long nor short: in poems equal in length to the average Hebrew psalm, the average Greek ode. No doubt there are exceptions: 'Sohrab and Rustum' among the longer poems, 'Requiescat' among the shorter, are nearly faultless. But, for the most part, it is in such poems as 'Thyrsis', 'A Summer Night', 'Stanzas from the Grande Chartreuse', that we find the true Arnold; not in 'Balder Dead', 'Progress', 'Revolutions'. In other words, Arnold, to use his own phrase, had not 'the architectonics of poetry, the faculty which presides at the evolution of works like the *Agamemnon* or *Lear*'. Nor was he in the literal sense a singer, such as was Heine or Catullus. Rather, his quality was meditative; he accepted, at least in practice, Wordsworth's definition of poetry, that it is 'emotion remembered in tranquillity'. But it may be objected that Arnold is genial, exultant, even rapturous; that he wrote nothing in the least like 'The Excursion'. That is true; but let us consider a little more curiously. Arnold was fond of national distinctions, qualities of race and temperament. Were one to distinguish Arnold's own qualities, the conclusion might be of this kind. From the Greek culture, he took a delight in the beauty of life and of fine imagination; from the Hebrew genius, a sense of reverence and meditation: from the French, a certain grace and lucidity of spirit; from the German, a steady seriousness of mind. By descent he was, in part, a Celt: that gave him a 'natural magic' of emotion and of soul; while from his English origin he took that daring common-sense which enabled him to hold in harmony these various qualities. Trained in those chosen places of beauty and high tradition, Winchester and Oxford, with all the strength of his father's influence at Rugby, he was always attached to the English ideal: to the ideals of Milton and of Burke. A scholar, a man of the world, a government official, his affections were not narrow, not provincial; but they were not cosmopolitan, not unsettled. His heart was at home in the quiet dignity and peace of an English life, among the great books of antiquity, and the great thoughts of 'all time and all existence'. Hence came his limitations: not from prejudice, nor from ignorance, but from a scrupulous precision and delicacy of taste. No one loved France more than he; no one abhorred more than he 'the great goddess Aselgeia'. He reverenced the German seriousness, depth, moderation of life and thought; he disliked and ridiculed pedantry, awkwardness, want of humour and of grace. In all his criticisms, the same balance between excess and deficiency appears: he was a true Aristotelian. And so, when it is said that Arnold was not a poet of profound philosophy, not a thinker of consistency, or not a man whom we can classify at all, the only answer is a *distinguo*. It was Arnold's work to find beauty and truth in life, to apprehend the meaning and moral worth of things, to discriminate the trivial from the grave, and to show how the serene and ardent life is better than the mean and restless. His poetry, then, is not didactic; but meditative, in the classical sense, it is. Lord Coleridge—in those papers which make us regret that he has 'to law given up what was meant for mankind',—is of opinion that Arnold's meditative poems are not destined to live, 'not from any defect of their own, but from the in-

herent mortality of their subjects'. Yet, surely these poems
are more than records of a transitory emotion, the phase and
habit of an age. Such a description would apply to Clough:
his mournful, homesick, desultory poems are indeed touched
with decay, because they are composed without care, in no
wide spirit of contemplation; reading them we do not think
of 'Sophocles by the Aegean', nor of the *lacrimae rerum.*
But Arnold's thoughts and emotions are profoundly human;
we cannot say of them that only an Oxford man, under such
and such influences, at such and such a time, could have felt
them in youth and expressed them in after-life. True, their
immediate tone is that of one 'touched by the Zeit-Geist' in
the latter end of the nineteenth century; but their fundamental character is common to all times. For Arnold is
human; and what is humanism but the belief

'that nothing which has ever interested living men and women
can wholly lose its vitality: no language they have spoken, no
oracle beside which they have hushed their voices, no dream
which has once been entertained by actual human minds, nothing about which they have ever been passionate, or expended
time and zeal'?

Arnold, if this be so, was himself a true humanist; and no
true humanist will ever forget him. No doubt the *Christian
Year* or the *Essay on Man* have lost their charm and their
significance; but we read the one as the memorial of a great
phase of sentiment, and the other for its brilliant setting of
a very tarnished theory. Much more will Arnold live in these
grave and lovely poems, which have so little in them of mere
transient feeling. Whatever be the future estimate of
Arnold's poems, there is no doubt of their singular charm
now. They possess the secret of great verse, its power of
haunting the memory, and of profoundly satisfying it. Sad
as are some of them, their melancholy is true to nature, and
leaves us calm; rejoicing as are others, they never soar out
of sight, away from life. But they give a view of nature and

of life as contemplated by a mind of great sympathy and insight, acquainted with the choice spirits of ancient civility, and with the living emotions of our own age. No hymn to Dolores can so touch us as the lines 'To Marguerite': the feverish, antiquarian rhetoric of the one may thrill the nerves and leave us tired; the pure beauty and the austere passion of the other appeals to every faculty in us, and leaves a sense of the beauty of human sorrow. Paradoxical as it may sound, there is something very hieratic about Arnold: his apprehension of the beauty of holiness, his love for what is clear and lofty in the pleasures of thought, his constant service of meditation.

> 'Ah, les Voix, mourez donc, mourantes que vous êtes:
> Sentences, mots en vain, métaphores mal faites,
> Toute la rhétorique en fuite des péchés,
> Ah, les Voix, mourez donc, mourantes que vous êtes!'

Arnold would not have liked M. Verlaine's poetry; but those lines express much of Arnold's mind. The false worship of words, the conventional acceptance of phrases, all the spurious wisdom in the world, he fought against, and conquered much of it; and there is no one left to take his place in the struggle against vulgarity and imposture: no voice like his to sing as he sang of calm and peace among the turbulent sounds of modern life.

H. W. GARROD

From *Poetry and the Criticism of Life* (1931)

SOHRAB AND RUSTUM is less a poem than the fragment of one. Indeed, if it be a poem, it is the only poem in the world that begins in the middle of a sentence:

> And the first grey of morning filled the east.

It marks, for Matthew Arnold, the first grey of a new poetical morn which, in fact, never grew to any settled glory of noonday power. Yet I ought not to speak of 'the first grey'; for the lights are, if sober, singularly pure; with a rather cold purity, if you like (I do not know), yet diffusing broadly the feeling air of a reserved dawn.

The poem gives us, not a story, but an episode: of which the culminating moment is presented with a grave art consciously reminiscent of Greek tragedy. Both Sohrab and his father are such personages as, from their position and character, satisfy the most exacting tragic canons; and the death of Sohrab at the hands of his father, by a deed of mere ignorance, offers a situation of that kind which the somewhat intellectualised drama of the Greeks was specially interested to illustrate. Upon the tragic act follows the recognition of what has been done. Here was that part of a Greek drama upon which the dramatist spent always his best pains. An essential element of almost any Attic tragedy, it was the 'recognition scene' which afforded to the tragedian his best opportunity of originality. In Matthew Arnold's poem the recognition is elaborated with peculiar art. The discovery of Sohrab by his father is contrived, it is true, by means of 'tokens'; a tragic artifice deprecated, or half-deprecated, by Aristotle. Sohrab is finally known by the tattoo marks which he bears pricked upon his arm. This was given to Matthew Arnold in the story as he found it. Yet even this weakness, if it be one, he has ingeniously—and by that I mean, with a fine poetic instinct—converted into a special kind of strength. Rustum recognizes his son by tokens. But for Sohrab's recognition of his father no tokens are used, none are required; the romantic heart of youth never asks logical proofs. In the moment when his nameless foe shouts at him Rustum's name, Sohrab *knows* that it is his father; the flash of recognition in which the knowledge comes to him is, in fact, his undoing—for a moment his eye falls, and he is exposed to Rustum's spear-thrust. The heart and eye of Rustum

are old and sceptical, *he* requires proofs; and the two
characters stand here delicately contrasted. Yet even
Rustum, we are made to feel, though he asks tokens, does
not really want them. All the while all the flesh in him had
been crying out 'O boy, thy father!'

The tragic manner, studied out of Sophocles in especial,
is diversified by beauties fetched from epic tradition;
beauties surely Virgilian rather than Homeric, though they
are meant, I fancy, to recall Homer. Some of them, indeed,
in their diffuse and soft and rather modern manner seem
to belong less to epic than to epic idyll, to that species
known to the Alexandrians as the *epyllion*. I am thinking
in particular of what are sometimes called the long-tailed
similes. Some critics find in *Sohrab* too much of this
ornament. But gentler spirits (among whom I would
wish to be) may be forgiven if they tire less easily of
beautiful images, and are not disposed to fret too much
over what element they may contain of the irrelevant and
adventitious:

>   And he saw that youth,
> Of age and looks to be his own dear son,
> Piteous and lovely, lying on the sand,
> Like some rich hyacinth which by the scythe
> Of an unskilful gardener has been cut,
> Mowing the garden grass-plots near its bed,
> And lies, a fragrant tower of purple bloom,
> On the mown, dying grass—so Sohrab lay,
> Lovely in death, upon the common sand . . .

The simile, there, of the hyacinth is, I suppose, in some
form or other, world-old. Old too may be, for all I know,
the simile of the violets, with whose 'soiled tissue' is
likened the wound in Sohrab's side:

> Like the soiled tissue of white violets
> Left, freshly gathered, on their native bank,
> By children whom their nurses call with haste
> Indoors from the sun's eye . . .

—yet the children called indoors by their nurses bring something that I do not recollect from elsewhere. It is a serious thing for a poet to try to be like Homer; a still more serious thing to try to improve upon him. Out of both adventures Matthew Arnold comes off, I fancy, more than once with credit:

> And now all strength was ebbed, and from his limbs
> Unwillingly the spirit fled away,
> Regretting the warm mansion that it left,
> And youth, and bloom, and this delightful world.

There are four lines that recall, as they were meant to do, two famous lines of Homer. They have an air more soft and modern than Homer's lines, the rhythm dropping to the languorous; and there will be severe scholars who will like them less on that account; and less, in any case, than Homer's lines. From that severity of scholarship I ask leave to stand aside.

But the poem is greatest in that passage of it which, if the poet had been either Homer or Sophocles, if he had wished to obey any rules there may be either for tragic or for epic art, would not have been there at all; I mean, of course, the last eighteen lines of it. I will not say that the passage is too well known to quote; I have the hope that, because you know it, you will be willing to bear with it again. Keep before you the picture, and what has preceded. 'On the bloody sand Sohrab lies dead.' Rustum draws his cloak over his face, and sits by his dead son. You might think them two black granite pillars, 'once high-reared By Jemshid in Persepolis,' now 'prone, enormous.' Awhile the two armies stand at gaze; over the solemn waste slowly night descends, and the fog rises up off the Oxus. Then camp-fires are kindled, and over the plain is borne the hum of the dispersing armies; presently Rustum and his son are left alone on the field:

But the majestic river floated on,
Out of the mist and hum of that low land,
Into the frosty starlight, and there moved,
Rejoicing, through the hushed Chorasmian waste,
Under the solitary moon;—he flowed
Right for the polar star, past Orgunje,
Brimming, and bright, and large; then sands begin
To hem his watery march, and dam his streams,
And split his currents; that for many a league
The shorn and parcelled Oxus strains along
Through beds of sand and matted rushy isles—
Oxus, forgetting the bright speed he had
In his high mountain-cradle in Pamere,
A foiled circuitous wanderer—till at last
The longed-for dash of waves is heard, and wide
His luminous home óf waters opens, bright
And tranquil, from whose floor the new-bathed stars
Emerge, and shine upon the Aral sea.

So the poem ends; and to epic or tragic art, those last
lines are vanity. I think them, none the less, not relevant
merely, but an essential part of the poem to which they
belong; upon the tragedy that has gone before, the perfect,
and only possible, commentary.

To the sticklers for *kinds* in poetry, I will confess plainly
that I do not know just to what kind to relegate *Sohrab and
Rustum*. But, if I did, of that kind, I would say, it is the
faultless example. You may like some other kind better,
you may seek qualities which this poem has not, different
and perhaps deeper qualities of the spirit; but you will not
easily find work more perfect, more instinct with harmony
and proportion, the parts of it more truly fused. Just what
he set himself to do in this poem, Matthew Arnold has done,
not less, nor more. If he had been questioned about it, I
think he would have said, leaving aside all bother about
kinds, that throughout the greater part of it he had en-
deavoured to carry to a modern reader some sense of the
qualities that distinguish Sophoclean art: selective power

in the disposition of a noble and moving story, a diction pitched to the grave quality of the theme, restraint both emotional and verbal, the harmonisation of all the elements of composition. This would touch only a part of the effects which characterise the poem: but a part not insignificant. Take that part, assume the purpose to be as I give it; what the poem seeks to do, it does with that degree of success which gives it a unique station in English poetry. *Sola Sophocleo tua carmina digna cothurno.*

I think it must please Matthew Arnold's ghost that the MS. of this poem, written in his own hand—a scholarly calligraphy—has its home to-day in Wordsworth's cottage in Grasmere. . . .

The range of Matthew Arnold's interests was wide. Leave aside his defect of history—which is patent—and forget his contempt for science; not merely in literature, but in education, in politics, in religion, he was deeply interested and well informed. Literature was, I suppose, his first love; but if he had stayed there, he would not have been, I am inclined to think, a better critic than some others. Unless I mistake, it is precisely the interest which he had in education, politics, and religion which makes his criticism original. The value of literature lay, he supposed, in its power to furnish a temper of mind; to create that dis-interested habit of intellect which secures for ideas a free play. Education, politics, religion, are immensely important subjects; to bring to them, not the prepossessions of ped-antry, nor party spirit, nor fanaticism—all of which proceed from either ignorance or narrowness—but to set playing on these subjects minds habituated to free or liberal motions, minds nursed on ideas, minds informed by the best that has been known and thought among men—this is what is everywhere wanted, this is that soul's salvation which literature, and literature only, can work out in us. Of all that Matthew Arnold says upon Criticism that is the main substance. It is said with the most plainness and vigour in the first of the *Essays in Criticism*; but all the other essays say it again, or they say nothing. Something like it, of course, is said by other critics; something like it is said whenever the claim of ideas is pressed against the tyranny of any materialism. But the energy and bright persuasiveness with which Matthew Arnold urges his cause, the skill of temper which he lends to his plea, the variety with which he illustrates his single thesis—these things make him original.

The study of literature ends in a disposition of mind; its best gift to us is some faculty of spiritual freedom, a certain largeness of temper. No one, perhaps,—not even the mere aesthetician,—will be much disposed to quarrel with that. But Matthew Arnold goes somewhat further than that. He valued literature, I think, just in proportion as it creates the temper in which to view the great interests of life. He is not, I fancy, quite consistent with himself. Sometimes, for example, he seems to think of poetry as though its first business were to furnish anodynes for life. Occasionally, he concedes to it some rather sober power of joy. Very rarely, perhaps never in his heart, does he think of it as a pure source of pleasure, a delight among other delights. In the main, as I say, he values literature for the temper which it teaches—poetry a temper of heart, prose a temper of the intellect; in either kind, the temper for looking at the great interests of life. For Matthew Arnold the great interests of life are the social and political and the religious. I think we too much forget how strong the obsession was with him, not merely of the religious interest, but of politics and the theory of society. Often enough, I know, he runs from politics—even from religion—to the consolations of poetry. Yet more often you might suppose him interested in literature only for its power to fit a man to judge questions of religion and social life. Indeed, if I am to mark him off as a

critic from other critics, to find that in him which is individual, I can best do it, I think, by saying that beyond
any other man of letters he valued the temper of the man
of letters—conceiving it, not as an end in itself, but as an
instrument of the art of living. . . .

As a critic of literature I rate him, after all deductions
made, very high. Some of the deductions that have to be
made I have already hinted, and others are obvious. I am
not prepared to break my heart over the fact that he is not
what is called a scientific critic. I am not offended by the
circumstance that he not only shows no interest in, but in
fact deprecates the use of, the historical method—the
master-discovery of his age. I am not offended by it; nor
surprised at it; for the truth is that Matthew Arnold was
not a learned man—that was why he sometimes talked as
though he knew everything. But he knew very little about
the history of literature, and he liked to think (what may
be true) that great poetry drops from the skies. In general,
he indulges too much the appeal to absolute standards. He
can as little tolerate that criticism should be personal as that
it should be historical; and he loses a good deal here in
warmth and colour. It is a habit of great poets, i.e., romantic poets, to seem not to belong to the world of books—
to seem out of keeping with the serenities and decorums of
literature. Expatiating in the Sacred Grove of poetry,
Matthew Arnold hated to see human faces peeping out at
him from behind the leaves—you could never tell when
human nature, or the poetic nature, was not going to be
malign, or even disreputable. Even so, he is not always
consistent with himself; and in fact some of his best
sketches are those in which the element of biography finds
a place.

It is in a different way, I think, that Matthew Arnold
disappoints us most. He thinks too much of the uses of
literature, and too little of its pleasures. He attaches too

much importance to taste, and too little to relish. By the waters of Helicon he sits down and sips, sampling them with the meticulous satisfaction of the wine-taster. It is horrible to see him, sometimes, tasting without swallowing. Nor in general has he, in appreciation, what I may call a good social manner. His criticism is tainted with a certain snobbery and even dandyism. All that is the defect, none the less, of a very real quality in him—he did believe in the best, and he did know that it was not the shoddy. Most of us do not; really, most critics do not. Matthew Arnold's genuine flair for the best, the insistency of his faith in the best, his pleasant manner of sharing it only with the best men—a secret between you and him—these are first-rate virtues; and not the less effective for an element which they have of the *stagy*. For there *is* a good deal of the poseur in him— I not only concede it cheerfully, but, to be honest, I enjoy it. I like the good art of it, and the supercilious airy amiability with which it is managed. If Matthew Arnold carried into political and social criticism the manner of a man of letters, he also carried into the criticism of literature —or liked to think that he did—the air of a man of the world. The rôle afforded him artistic delight; and on the whole it was well suited to him. The part of it which he carries least well is the cosmopolitan pose, the affectation of being born on the continent. But in general his bland finish of manner, and the delicacy of his irony, are beyond praise. If he is not the greatest of English critics, his make-up of being so is in itself a piece of greatness; and not to enjoy it is a piece of stupidity.

Indeed, Matthew Arnold's real distinction, and the best hope for him of a permanent fame in criticism, is that he is so extraordinarily enjoyable. He is enjoyable almost everywhere; and a part of the enjoyment is, if we are honest with ourselves, the delight which we derive from a finely adjusted pose. I am not sure that we have not too much

outgrown what I would call the simpler pleasures of literature—it is part and parcel of a general sophistication. But
I will not be put off by it. Because others are sophisticated,
I am not going to be ashamed to say that, after the fashion
of the period in which I was born, I value literature very
largely by the enjoyment which I derive from it. I am
delighted in Matthew Arnold by what I feel to be the
pervasive charm of his temper—it is not the less charming
to me from the affectations that go with it. The style of
mind, the manner, delights me—as an artistic product it
delights me. And yet again, and finally, and yet more in
the fashion of yesterday, I enjoy above all things Matthew
Arnold's beautiful English. Here again, some affectations
that I am aware of do not hurt me—I think they enhance
my satisfactions. Perhaps Matthew Arnold's style a little
lacks masculinity; at least the he-men of literature do not
write like this. Yet it has qualities which we shall be hard
put to it to match in any others of our prose-writers. For
a like delicacy of prose-style, for a prose equally character-
ized by symmetry and proportion and harmony, we are
driven to French literature or to the ancient Greek. I hate
to speak of truth of style—it opens the floodgates for bad
metaphysic or for cant. But, properly guarded, the phrase
does mean something. In Matthew Arnold's beautiful
English I seem to myself always to find both grace and
truth. Grace and truth are qualities rare, I suppose, in any
age. Our own age wants grace perhaps more than truth.
We *have* a kind of ugly truthfulness. But we too little
esteem grace—and we have ceased to read Matthew Arnold.

Selections from
MATTHEW ARNOLD

SHAKESPEARE

1844. The Strayed Reveller (1849)

OTHERS abide our question. Thou art free.
We ask and ask—Thou smilest and art still,
Out-topping knowledge. For the loftiest hill,
Who to the stars uncrowns his majesty,

Planting his steadfast footsteps in the sea,   5
Making the heaven of heavens his dwelling-place,
Spares but the cloudy border of his base
To the foil'd searching of mortality;

And thou, who didst the stars and sunbeams know,
Self-school'd, self-scann'd, self-honour'd, self-secure, 10
Didst tread on earth unguess'd at.—Better so!

All pains the immortal spirit must endure,
All weakness which impairs, all griefs which bow,
Find their sole speech in that victorious brow.

TO A FRIEND

The Strayed Reveller (1849)

WHO prop, thou ask'st, in these bad days, my mind?—
He much, the old man, who, clearest-soul'd of men,
Saw The Wide Prospect, and the Asian Fen,
And Tmolus hill, and Smyrna bay, though blind.

Much he, whose friendship I not long since won,   5
That halting slave, who in Nicopolis
Taught Arrian, when Vespasian's brutal son
Clear'd Rome of what most shamed him. But be his

My special thanks, whose even-balanced soul,
From first youth tested up to extreme old age,   10
Business could not make dull, nor passion wild;

Who saw life steadily, and saw it whole;
The mellow glory of the Attic stage,
Singer of sweet Colonus, and its child.

THE FORSAKEN MERMAN

The Strayed Reveller (1849)

COME, dear children, let us away;
Down and away below!
Now my brothers call from the bay,
Now the great winds shoreward blow,
Now the salt tides seaward flow;   5
Now the wild white horses play,
Champ and chafe and toss in the spray.
Children dear, let us away!
This way, this way!

Call her once before you go—   10
Call once yet!
In a voice that she will know:
'Margaret! Margaret!'
Children's voices should be dear
(Call once more) to a mother's ear;   15
Children's voices, wild with pain—
Surely she will come again!
Call her once and come away;
This way, this way!
'Mother dear, we cannot stay!   20
The wild white horses foam and fret.'
Margaret! Margaret!

Come, dear children, come away down;
Call no more!
One last look at the white-wall'd town, 25
And the little grey church on the windy shore;
Then come down!
She will not come though you call all day;
Come away, come away!

Children dear, was it yesterday 30
We heard the sweet bells over the bay?
In the caverns where we lay,
Through the surf and through the swell,
The far-off sound of a silver bell?
Sand-strewn caverns, cool and deep, 35
Where the winds are all asleep;
Where the spent lights quiver and gleam,
Where the salt weed sways in the stream,
Where the sea-beasts, ranged all round,
Feed in the ooze of their pasture-ground; 40
Where the sea-snakes coil and twine,
Dry their mail and bask in the brine;
Where great whales come sailing by,
Sail and sail, with unshut eye,
Round the world for ever and aye? 45
When did music come this way?
Children dear, was it yesterday?

Children dear, was it yesterday
(Call yet once) that she went away?
Once she sate with you and me, 50
On a red gold throne in the heart of the sea,
And the youngest sate on her knee.
She comb'd its bright hair, and she tended it well,
When down swung the sound of a far-off bell.
She sigh'd, she look'd up through the clear green sea; 55

She said: 'I must go, for my kinsfolk pray
In the little grey church on the shore to-day.
'Twill be Easter-time in the world—ah me!
And I lose my poor soul, Merman! here with thee.'
I said: 'Go up, dear heart, through the waves;   60
Say thy prayer, and come back to the kind sea-caves!'
She smiled, she went up through the surf in the bay.
Children dear, was it yesterday?

Children dear, were we long alone?
'The sea grows stormy, the little ones moan;   65
Long prayers,' I said, 'in the world they say;
Come!' I said; and we rose through the surf in the bay.
We went up the beach, by the sandy down
Where the sea-stocks bloom, to the white-wall'd town;
Through the narrow paved streets, where all was still,   70
To the little grey church on the windy hill.
From the church came a murmur of folk at their prayers,
But we stood without in the cold blowing airs.
We climb'd on the graves, on the stones worn with rains,
And we gazed up the aisle through the small leaded panes.
She sate by the pillar; we saw her clear: 76
'Margaret, hist! come quick, we are here!
Dear heart,' I said, 'we are long alone;
The sea grows stormy, the little ones moan.'
But, ah, she gave me never a look,   80
For her eyes were seal'd to the holy book!
Loud prays the priest; shut stands the door.
Come away, children, call no more!
Come away, come down, call no more!

Down, down, down!   85
Down to the depths of the sea!
She sits at her wheel in the humming town,
Singing most joyfully.
Hark what she sings: 'O joy, O joy,

For the humming street, and the child with its toy! 90
For the priest, and the bell, and the holy well;
For the wheel where I spun,
And the blessed light of the sun!'
And so she sings her fill,
Singing most joyfully, 95
Till the spindle drops from her hand,
And the whizzing wheel stands still.
She steals to the window, and looks at the sand,
And over the sand at the sea;
And her eyes are set in a stare; 100
And anon there breaks a sigh,
And anon there drops a tear,
From a sorrow-clouded eye,
And a heart sorrow-laden,
A long, long sigh; 105
For the cold strange eyes of a little Mermaiden
And the gleam of her golden hair.

  Come away, away children;
Come children, come down!
The hoarse wind blows coldly; 110
Lights shine in the town.
She will start from her slumber
When gusts shake the door;
She will hear the winds howling,
Will hear the waves roar. 115
We shall see, while above us
The waves roar and whirl,
A ceiling of amber,
A pavement of pearl.
Singing: 'Here came a mortal, 120
But faithless was she!
And alone dwell for ever
The kings of the sea.'

But, children, at midnight,
When soft the winds blow,   125
When clear falls the moonlight,
When spring-tides are low;
When sweet airs come seaward
From heaths starr'd with broom,
And high rocks throw mildly   130
On the blanch'd sands a gloom;
Up the still, glistening beaches,
Up the creeks we will hie,
Over banks of bright seaweed
The ebb-tide leaves dry.   135
We will gaze, from the sand-hills,
At the white, sleeping town;
At the church on the hill-side—
And then come back down.
Singing: 'There dwells a loved one,   140
But cruel is she!
She left lonely for ever
The kings of the sea.'

RESIGNATION

TO FAUSTA

The Strayed Reveller (1849)

To die be given us, or attain!
Fierce work it were, to do again.
So pilgrims, bound for Mecca, pray'd
At burning noon; so warriors said,
Scarf'd with the cross, who watch'd the miles   5
Of dust which wreathed their struggling files
Down Lydian mountains; so, when snows
Round Alpine summits, eddying, rose,

The Goth, bound Rome-wards; so the Hun,
Crouch'd on his saddle, while the sun   10
Went lurid down o'er flooded plains
Through which the groaning Danube strains
To the drear Euxine;—so pray all,
Whom labours, self-ordain'd, enthrall;
Because they to themselves propose   15
On this side the all-common close
A goal which, gain'd, may give repose.
So pray they; and to stand again
Where they stood once, to them were pain;
Pain to thread back and to renew   20
Past straits, and currents long steer'd through.

But milder natures, and more free—
Whom an unblamed serenity
Hath freed from passions, and the state
Of struggle these necessitate;   25
Whom schooling of the stubborn mind
Hath made, or birth hath found, resign'd—
These mourn not, that their goings pay
Obedience to the passing day.
These claim not every laughing Hour   30
For handmaid to their striding power;
Each in her turn, with torch uprear'd,
To await their march; and when appear'd,
Through the cold gloom, with measured race,
To usher for a destined space   35
(Her own sweet errands all forgone)
The too imperious traveller on.
These, Fausta, ask not this; nor thou,
Time's chafing prisoner, ask it now!

We left, just ten years since, you say,   40
That wayside inn we left to-day.

Our jovial host, as forth we fare,
Shouts greeting from his easy chair.
High on a bank our leader stands,
Reviews and ranks his motley bands,   45
Makes clear our goal to every eye—
The valley's western boundary.
A gate swings to! our tide hath flow'd
Already from the silent road.
The valley-pastures, one by one,   50
Are threaded, quiet in the sun;
And now beyond the rude stone bridge
Slopes gracious up the western ridge.
Its woody border, and the last
Of its dark upland farms is past—   55
Cool farms, with open-lying stores,
Under their burnish'd sycamores;
All past! and through the trees we glide,
Emerging on the green hill-side.
There climbing hangs, a far-seen sign,   60
Our wavering, many-colour'd line;
There winds, upstreaming slowly still
Over the summit of the hill.
And now, in front, behold outspread
Those upper regions we must tread!   65
Mild hollows, and clear healthy swells,
The cheerful silence of the fells.
Some two hours' march with serious air,
Through the deep noontide heats we fare;
The red-grouse, springing at our sound,   70
Skims, now and then, the shining ground;
No life, save his and ours, intrudes
Upon these breathless solitudes.
O joy! again the farms appear.
Cool shade is there, and rustic cheer;   75
There springs the brook will guide us down,

Bright comrade, to the noisy town.
Lingering, we follow down; we gain
The town, the highway, and the plain.
And many a mile of dusty way,   80
Parch'd and road-worn, we made that day;
But, Fausta, I remember well,
That as the balmy darkness fell
We bathed our hands with speechless glee,
That night, in the wide-glimmering sea.   85

Once more we tread this self-same road,
Fausta, which ten years since we trod;
Alone we tread it, you and I,
Ghosts of that boisterous company.
Here, where the brook shines, near its head,   90
In its clear, shallow, turf-fringed bed;
Here, whence the eye first sees, far down,
Capp'd with faint smoke, the noisy town;
Here sit we, and again unroll,
Though slowly, the familiar whole.   95
The solemn wastes of heathy hill
Sleep in the July sunshine still;
The self-same shadows now, as then,
Play through this grassy upland glen;
The loose dark stones on the green way   100
Lie strewn, it seems, where then they lay;
On this mild bank above the stream,
(You crush them!) the blue gentians gleam.
Still this wild brook, the rushes cool,
The sailing foam, the shining pool!   105
These are not changed; and we, you say,
Are scarce more changed, in truth, than they.

The gipsies, whom we met below,
They, too, have long roam'd to and fro;

They ramble, leaving, where they pass,   110
Their fragments on the cumber'd grass.
And often to some kindly place
Chance guides the migratory race,
Where, though long wanderings intervene,
They recognise a former scene.   115
The dingy tents are pitch'd; the fires
Give to the wind their wavering spires;
In dark knots crouch round the wild flame
Their children, as when first they came;
They see their shackled beasts again   120
Move, browsing, up the gray-wall'd lane.
Signs are not wanting, which might raise
The ghost in them of former days—
Signs are not wanting, if they would;
Suggestions to disquietude.   125
For them, for all, time's busy touch,
While it mends little, troubles much.
Their joints grow stiffer—but the year
Runs his old round of dubious cheer;
Chilly they grow—yet winds in March,   130
Still, sharp as ever, freeze and parch;
They must live still—and yet, God knows,
Crowded and keen the country grows;
It seems as if, in their decay,
The law grew stronger every day.   135
So might they reason, so compare,
Fausta, times past with times that are.
But no!—they rubb'd through yesterday
In their hereditary way,
And they will rub through, if they can,   140
To-morrow on the self-same plan,
Till death arrive to supersede,
For them, vicissitude and need.

The poet, to whose mighty heart
Heaven doth a quicker pulse impart,   145
Subdues that energy to scan
Not his own course, but that of man.
Though he move mountains, though his day
Be pass'd on the proud heights of sway,
Though he hath loosed a thousand chains,   150
Though he hath borne immortal pains,
Action and suffering though he know—
He hath not lived, if he lives so.
He sees, in some great-historied land,
A ruler of the people stand,   155
Sees his strong thought in fiery flood
Roll through the heaving multitude,
Exults—yet for no moment's space
Envies the all-regarded place.
Beautiful eyes meet his—and he   160
Bears to admire uncravingly;
They pass—he, mingled with the crowd,
Is in their far-off triumphs proud.
From some high station he looks down,
At sunset, on a populous town;   165
Surveys each happy group, which fleets,
Toil ended, through the shining streets,
Each with some errand of its own—
And does not say: *I am alone.*
He sees the gentle stir of birth   170
When morning purifies the earth;
He leans upon a gate and sees
The pastures, and the quiet trees.
Low, woody hill, with gracious bound,
Folds the still valley almost round;   175
The cuckoo, loud on some high lawn,
Is answer'd from the depth of dawn;
In the hedge straggling to the stream,

Pale, dew-drench'd, half-shut roses gleam;
But, where the farther side slopes down,   180
He sees the drowsy new-waked clown
In his white quaint-embroider'd frock
Make, whistling, tow'rd his mist-wreathed flock—
Slowly, behind his heavy tread,
The wet, flower'd grass heaves up its head.   185
Lean'd on his gate, he gazes—tears
Are in his eyes, and in his ears
The murmur of a thousand years.
Before him he sees life unroll,
A placid and continuous whole—   190
That general life, which does not cease,
Whose secret is not joy, but peace;
That life, whose dumb wish is not miss'd
If birth proceeds, if things subsist;
The life of plants, and stones, and rain,   195
The life he craves—if not in vain
Fate gave, what chance shall not control,
His sad lucidity of soul.

You listen—but that wandering smile,
Fausta, betrays you cold the while!   200
Your eyes pursue the bells of foam
Wash'd, eddying, from this bank, their home.
Those gipsies, so your thoughts I scan,
Are less, the poet more, than man.
They feel not, though they move and see;   205
Deeper the poet feels; but he
Breathes, when he will, immortal air,
Where Orpheus and where Homer are.
In the day's life, whose iron round
Hems us all in, he is not bound;   210
He leaves his kind, o'erleaps their pen,
And flees the common life of men.

He escapes thence, but we abide—
Not deep the poet sees, but wide.

The world in which we live and move   215
Outlasts aversion, outlasts love,
Outlasts each effort, interest, hope,
Remorse, grief, joy;—and were the scope
Of these affections wider made,
Man still would see, and see dismay'd,   220
Beyond his passion's widest range,
Far regions of eternal change.
Nay, and since death, which wipes out man,
Finds him with many an unsolved plan,
With much unknown, and much untried,   225
Wonder not dead, and thirst not dried,
Still gazing on the ever full
Eternal mundane spectacle—
This world in which we draw our breath,
In some sense, Fausta, outlasts death.   230
Blame thou not, therefore, him who dares
Judge vain beforehand human cares;
Whose natural insight can discern
What through experience others learn;
Who needs not love and power, to know   235
Love transient, power an unreal show;
Who treads at ease life's uncheer'd ways—
Him blame not, Fausta, rather praise!
Rather thyself for some aim pray
Nobler than this, to fill the day;   240
Rather that heart, which burns in thee,
Ask, not to amuse, but to set free;
Be passionate hopes not ill resign'd
For quiet, and a fearless mind.
And though fate grudge to thee and me   245
The poet's rapt security,

Yet they, believe me, who await
No gifts from chance, have conquer'd fate.
They, winning room to see and hear,
And to men's business not too near,   250
Through clouds of individual strife
Draw homeward to the general life.
Like leaves by suns not yet uncurl'd;
To the wise, foolish; to the world,
Weak;—yet not weak, I might reply,   255
Not foolish, Fausta, in His eye,
To whom each moment in its race,
Crowd as we will its neutral space,
Is but a quiet watershed   259
Whence, equally, the seas of life and death are fed.

Enough, we live!—and if a life,
With large results so little rife,
Though bearable, seem hardly worth
This pomp of worlds, this pain of birth;
Yet, Fausta, the mute turf we tread,   265
The solemn hills around us spread,
This stream which falls incessantly,
The strange-scrawl'd rocks, the lonely sky,
If I might lend their life a voice,
Seem to bear rather than rejoice.   270
And even could the intemperate prayer
Man iterates, while these forbear,
For movement, for an ampler sphere,
Pierce Fate's impenetrable ear;
Not milder is the general lot   275
Because our spirits have forgot,
In action's dizzying eddy whirl'd,
The something that infects the world.

ISOLATION. TO MARGUERITE

1849 ? *Poems* (1857)

WE were apart; yet, day by day,
I bade my heart more constant be.
I bade it keep the world away,
And grow a home for only thee;
Nor fear'd but thy love likewise grew,   5
Like mine, each day, more tried, more true.

The fault was grave! I might have known,
What far too soon, alas! I learn'd—
The heart can bind itself alone,
And faith may oft be unreturn'd.   10
Self-sway'd our feelings ebb and swell—
Thou lov'st no more;—Farewell! Farewell!

Farewell!—and thou, thou lonely heart,
Which never yet without remorse
Even for a moment didst depart   15
From thy remote and spheréd course
To haunt the place where passions reign—
Back to thy solitude again!

Back! with the conscious thrill of shame
Which Luna felt, that summer-night,   20
Flash through her pure immortal frame,
When she forsook the starry height
To hang over Endymion's sleep
Upon the pine-grown Latmian steep.

Yet she, chaste queen, had never proved   25
How vain a thing is mortal love,
Wandering in Heaven, far removed.
But thou hast long had place to prove

This truth—to prove, and make thine own:
'Thou hast been, shalt be, art, alone.'   30

Or, if not quite alone, yet they
Which touch thee are unmating things—
Ocean and clouds and night and day;
Lorn autumns and triumphant springs;
And life, and others' joy and pain,   35
And love, if love, of happier men.

Of happier men—for they, at least,
Have *dream'd* two human hearts might blend
In one, and were through faith released
From isolation without end   40
Prolong'd; nor knew, although not less
Alone than thou, their loneliness.

TO MARGUERITE—CONTINUED

1849? *Empedocles on Etna* (1852)

YES! in the sea of life enisled,
With echoing straits between us thrown,
Dotting the shoreless watery wild,
We mortal millions live *alone*.
The islands feel the enclasping flow,   5
And then their endless bounds they know.

But when the moon their hollows lights,
And they are swept by balms of spring,
And in their glens, on starry nights,
The nightingales divinely sing;   10
And lovely notes, from shore to shore,
Across the sounds and channels pour—

Oh! then a longing like despair
Is to their farthest caverns sent;
For surely once, they feel, we were   15
Parts of a single continent!
Now round us spreads the watery plain—
Oh might our marges meet again!

Who order'd, that their longing's fire
Should be, as soon as kindled, cool'd?   20
Who renders vain their deep desire?—
A God, a God their severance ruled!
And bade betwixt their shores to be
The unplumb'd, salt, estranging sea.

STANZAS IN MEMORY OF THE AUTHOR OF 'OBERMANN'

1849. *Empedocles on Etna* (1852)

In front the awful Alpine track
Crawls up its rocky stair;
The autumn storm-winds drive the rack,
Close o'er it, in the air.

Behind are the abandon'd baths   5
Mute in their meadows lone;
The leaves are on the valley-paths,
The mists are on the Rhone—

The white mists rolling like a sea!
I hear the torrents roar.   10
—Yes, Obermann, all speaks of thee;
I feel thee near once more!

I turn thy leaves! I feel their breath
Once more upon me roll;
That air of languor, cold, and death,   15
Which brooded o'er thy soul.

Fly hence, poor wretch, whoe'er thou art,
Condemn'd to cast about,
All shipwreck in thy own weak heart,
For comfort from without!   20

A fever in these pages burns
Beneath the calm they feign;
A wounded human spirit turns,
Here, on its bed of pain.

Yes, though the virgin mountain-air   25
Fresh through these pages blows;
Though to these leaves the glaciers spare
The soul of their white snows;

Though here a mountain-murmur swells
Of many a dark-bough'd pine;   30
Though, as you read, you hear the bells
Of the high-pasturing kine—

Yet, through the hum of torrent lone,
And brooding mountain-bee,
There sobs I know not what ground-tone   35
Of human agony.

Is it for this, because the sound
Is fraught too deep with pain,
That, Obermann! the world around
So little loves thy strain?   40

Some secrets may the poet tell,
For the world loves new ways;
To tell too deep ones is not well—
It knows not what he says.

Yet, of the spirits who have reign'd   45
In this our troubled day,
I know but two, who have attain'd,
Save thee, to see their way.

By England's lakes, in grey old age,
His quiet home one keeps;   50
And one, the strong much-toiling sage,
In German Weimar sleeps.

But Wordsworth's eyes avert their ken
From half of human fate;
And Goethe's course few sons of men   55
May think to emulate.

For he pursued a lonely road,
His eyes on Nature's plan;
Neither made man too much a God,
Nor God too much a man.   60

Strong was he, with a spirit free
From mists, and sane, and clear;
Clearer, how much! than ours—yet we
Have a worse course to steer.

For though his manhood bore the blast   65
Of a tremendous time,
Yet in a tranquil world was pass'd
His tenderer youthful prime.

But we, brought forth and rear'd in hours
Of change, alarm, surprise—   70
What shelter to grow ripe is ours?
What leisure to grow wise?

Like children bathing on the shore,
Buried a wave beneath,
The second wave succeeds, before   75
We have had time to breathe.

Too fast we live, too much are tried,
Too harass'd, to attain
Wordsworth's sweet calm, or Goethe's wide
And luminous view to gain.   80

And then we turn, thou sadder sage,
To thee! we feel thy spell!
—The hopeless tangle of our age,
Thou too hast scann'd it well!

Immoveable thou sittest, still   85
As death, composed to bear!
Thy head is clear, thy feeling chill,
And icy thy despair.

Yes, as the son of Thetis said,
I hear thee saying now: 90
Greater by far than thou art dead;
Strive not! die also thou!

Ah! two desires toss about
The poet's feverish blood.
One drives him to the world without,   95
And one to solitude.

The glow, he cries, *the thrill of life,*
Where, where do these abound?—
Not in the world, not in the strife
Of men, shall they be found.   100

He who hath watch'd, not shared, the strife,
Knows how the day hath gone.
He only lives with the world's life,
Who hath renounced his own.

To thee we come, then! Clouds are roll'd   105
Where thou, O seer! art set;
Thy realm of thought is drear and cold—
The world is colder yet!

And thou hast pleasures, too, to share
With those who come to thee—   110
Balms floating on thy mountain-air,
And healing sights to see.

How often, where the slopes are green
On Jaman, hast thou sate
By some high chalet-door, and seen   115
The summer-day grow late;

And darkness steal o'er the wet grass
With the pale crocus starr'd,
And reach that glimmering sheet of glass
Beneath the piny sward,   120

Lake Leman's waters, far below!
And watch'd the rosy light
Fade from the distant peaks of snow;
And on the air of night

Heard accents of the eternal tongue   125
Through the pine branches play—
Listen'd, and felt thyself grow young!
Listen'd and wept——Away!

Away the dreams that but deceive
And thou, sad guide, adieu!   130
I go, fate drives me; but I leave
Half of my life with you.

We, in some unknown Power's employ,
Move on a rigorous line;
Can neither, when we will, enjoy,   135
Nor, when we will, resign.

I in the world must live; but thou,
Thou melancholy shade!
Wilt not, if thou canst see me now,
Condemn me, nor upbraid.   140

For thou art gone away from earth,
And place with those dost claim,
The Children of the Second Birth,
Whom the world could not tame;

And with that small, transfigured band,   145
Whom many a different way
Conducted to their common land,
Thou learn'st to think as they.

Christian and pagan, king and slave,
Soldier and anchorite,   150
Distinctions we esteem so grave,
Are nothing in their sight.

They do not ask, who pined unseen,
Who was on action hurl'd,
Whose one bond is, that all have been   155
Unspotted by the world.

There without anger thou wilt see
Him who obeys thy spell
No more, so he but rest, like thee,
Unsoil'd!—and so, farewell.   160

Farewell!—Whether thou now liest near
That much-loved inland sea,
The ripples of whose blue waves cheer
Vevey and Meillerie:

And in that gracious region bland,   165
Where with clear-rustling wave
The scented pines of Switzerland
Stand dark round thy green grave,

Between the dusty vineyard-walls
Issuing on that green place   170
The early peasant still recalls
The pensive stranger's face,

And stoops to clear thy moss-grown date
Ere he plods on again ;—
Or whether, by maligner fate,   175
Among the swarms of men,

Where between granite terraces
The blue Seine rolls her wave,
The Capital of Pleasure sees
The hardly-heard-of grave ;—   180

Farewell! Under the sky we part,
In the stern Alpine dell.
O unstrung will! O broken heart!
A last, a last farewell!

MEMORIAL VERSES

1850. *Empedocles on Etna* (1852)

GOETHE in Weimar sleeps, and Greece,
Long since, saw Byron's struggle cease.
But one such death remain'd to come;
The last poetic voice is dumb—
We stand to-day by Wordsworth's tomb.   5

When Byron's eyes were shut in death,
We bow'd our head and held our breath.
He taught us little; but our soul
Had *felt* him like the thunder's roll.
With shivering heart the strife we saw   10
Of passion with eternal law;
And yet with reverential awe
We watch'd the fount of fiery life
Which served for that Titanic strife.

   When Goethe's death was told, we said: 15
Sunk, then, is Europe's sagest head.
Physician of the iron age,
Goethe has done his pilgrimage.
He took the suffering human race,
He read each wound, each weakness clear;   20
And struck his finger on the place,
And said: *Thou ailest here, and here!*
He look'd on Europe's dying hour

Of fitful dream and feverish power;
His eye plunged down the weltering strife,   25
The turmoil of expiring life—
He said: *The end is everywhere,*
Art still has truth, take refuge there!
And he was happy, if to know
Causes of things, and far below   30
His feet to see the lurid flow
Of terror, and insane distress,
And headlong fate, be happiness.

And Wordsworth!—Ah, pale ghosts, rejoice!
For never has such soothing voice   35
Been to your shadowy world convey'd,
Since erst, at morn, some wandering shade
Heard the clear song of Orpheus come
Through Hades, and the mournful gloom.
Wordsworth has gone from us—and ye,   40
Ah, may ye feel his voice as we!
He too upon a wintry clime
Had fallen—on this iron time
Of doubts, disputes, distractions, fears.
He found us when the age had bound   45
Our souls in its benumbing round;
He spoke, and loosed our heart in tears.
He laid us as we lay at birth
On the cool flowery lap of earth,
Smiles broke from us and we had ease;   50
The hills were round us, and the breeze
Went o'er the sun-lit fields again;
Our foreheads felt the wind and rain.
Our youth return'd; for there was shed
On spirits that had long been dead,   55
Spirits dried up and closely furl'd,
The freshness of the early world.

Ah! since dark days still bring to light
Man's prudence and man's fiery might,
Time may restore us in his course   60
Goethe's sage mind and Byron's force;
But where will Europe's latter hour
Again find Wordsworth's healing power?
Others will teach us how to dare,
And against fear our breast to steel;   65
Others will strengthen us to bear—
But who, ah! who, will make us feel?
The cloud of mortal destiny,
Others will front it fearlessly—
But who, like him, will put it by?   70

Keep fresh the grass upon his grave
O Rotha, with thy living wave!
Sing him thy best! for few or none
Hears thy voice right, now he is gone.

CADMUS AND HARMONIA

Empedocles on Etna (1852)

FAR, far from here,
The Adriatic breaks in a warm bay
Among the green Illyrian hills; and there
The sunshine in the happy glens is fair,
And by the sea, and in the brakes.   5
The grass is cool, the sea-side air
Buoyant and fresh, the mountain flowers
More virginal and sweet than ours.

And there, they say, two bright and aged snakes,
Who once were Cadmus and Harmonia,   10
Bask in the glens or on the warm sea-shore,
In breathless quiet, after all their ills;

Nor do they see their country, nor the place
Where the Sphinx lived among the frowning hills,
Nor the unhappy palace of their race,   15
Nor Thebes, nor the Ismenus, any more.

There those two live, far in the Illyrian brakes!
They had stay'd long enough to see,
In Thebes, the billow of calamity
Over their own dear children roll'd,   20
Curse upon curse, pang upon pang,
For years, they sitting helpless in their home,
A grey old man and woman; yet of old
The Gods had to their marriage come,
And at the banquet all the Muses sang.   25

Therefore they did not end their days
In sight of blood; but were rapt, far away,
To where the west-wind plays,
And murmurs of the Adriatic come
To those untrodden mountain-lawns; and there   30
Placed safely in changed forms, the pair
Wholly forget their first sad life, and home,
And all that Theban woe, and stray
For ever through the glens, placid and dumb.

APOLLO AND THE MUSES

Empedocles on Etna (1852)

THROUGH the black, rushing smoke-bursts,
Thick breaks the red flame;
All Etna heaves fiercely
Her forest-clothed frame.

Not here, O Apollo!   5
Are haunts meet for thee.
But, where Helicon breaks down
In cliff to the sea,

Where the moon-silver'd inlets
Send far their light voice   10
Up the still vale of Thisbe,
O speed, and rejoice!

On the sward at the cliff-top
Lie strewn the white flocks,
On the cliff-side the pigeons   15
Roost deep in the rocks.

In the moonlight the shepherds,
Soft lull'd by the rills,
Lie wrapt in their blankets
Asleep on the hills.   20

—What forms are these coming
So white through the gloom?
What garments out-glistening
The gold-flower'd broom?

What sweet-breathing presence   25
Out-perfumes the thyme?
What voices enrapture
The night's balmy prime?—

'Tis Apollo comes leading
His choir, the Nine.   30
—The leader is fairest,
But all are divine.

They are lost in the hollows!
They stream up again!
What seeks on this mountain   35
The glorified train?—

D

They bathe on this mountain,
In the spring by their road;
Then on to Olympus,
Their endless abode.   40

—Whose praise do they mention?
Of what is it told?—
What will be for ever;
What was from of old.

First hymn they the Father   45
Of all things; and then,
The rest of immortals,
The action of men.

The day in his hotness,
The strife with the palm;   50
The night in her silence,
The stars in their calm.

YOUTH AND CALM

Empedocles on Etna (1852), revised 1867

'Tis death! and peace, indeed, is here,
And ease from shame, and rest from fear.
There's nothing can dismarble now
The smoothness of that limpid brow.
But is a calm like this, in truth,   5
The crowning end of life and youth,
And when this boon rewards the dead,
Are all debts paid, has all been said?
And is the heart of youth so light,
Its step so firm, its eyes so bright,   10
Because on its hot brow there blows
A wind of promise and repose

From the far grave, to which it goes;
Because it hath the hope to come,
One day, to harbour in the tomb?   15
Ah no, the bliss youth dreams is one
For daylight, for the cheerful sun,
For feeling nerves and living breath—
Youth dreams a bliss on this side death.
It dreams a rest, if not more deep,   20
More grateful than this marble sleep;
It hears a voice within it tell:
Calm's not life's crown, though calm is well.
'Tis all perhaps which man acquires,
But 'tis not what our youth desires.   25

ISEULT OF BRITTANY

Empedocles on Etna (1852)

A YEAR had flown, and o'er the sea away,
In Cornwall, Tristram and Queen Iseult lay;
In King Marc's chapel, in Tyntagel old—
There in a ship they bore those lovers cold.

The young surviving Iseult, one bright day,   5
Had wander'd forth. Her children were at play
In a green circular hollow in the heath
Which borders the sea-shore—a country path
Creeps over it from the till'd fields behind.
The hollow's grassy banks are soft-inclined,   10
And to one standing on them, far and near
The lone unbroken view spreads bright and clear
Over the waste. This cirque of open ground
Is light and green; the heather, which all round
Creeps thickly, grows not here; but the pale grass 15

Is strewn with rocks, and many a shiver'd mass
Of vein'd white-gleaming quartz, and here and there
Dotted with holly-trees and juniper.
In the smooth centre of the opening stood
Three hollies side by side, and made a screen,   20
Warm with the winter-sun, of burnish'd green
With scarlet berries gemm'd, the fell-fare's food.
Under the glittering hollies Iseult stands,
Watching her children play; their little hands
Are busy gathering spars of quartz, and streams   25
Of stagshorn for their hats; anon, with screams
Of mad delight they drop their spoils, and bound
Among the holly-clumps and broken ground,
Racing full speed, and startling in their rush
The fell-fares and the speckled missel-thrush   30
Out of their glossy coverts;—but when now
Their cheeks were flush'd, and over each hot brow,
Under the feather'd hats of the sweet pair,
In blinding masses shower'd the golden hair—
Then Iseult call'd them to her, and the three   35
Cluster'd under the holly-screen, and she
Told them an old-world Breton history.

Warm in their mantles wrapt the three stood there,
Under the hollies, in the clear still air—
Mantles with those rich furs deep glistering   40
Which Venice ships do from swart Egypt bring.
Long they stay'd still—then, pacing at their ease,
Moved up and down under the glossy trees.
But still, as they pursued their warm dry road,
From Iseult's lips the unbroken story flow'd,   45
And still the children listen'd, their blue eyes
Fix'd on their mother's face in wide surprise;
Nor did their looks stray once to the sea-side,
Nor to the brown heaths round them, bright and wide,

Nor to the snow, which, though 't was all away   50
From the open heath, still by the hedgerows lay,
Nor to the shining sea-fowl, that with screams
Bore up from where the bright Atlantic gleams,
Swooping to landward; nor to where, quite clear,
The fell-fares settled on the thickets near.   55
And they would still have listen'd, till dark night
Came keen and chill down on the heather bright;
But, when the red glow on the sea grew cold,
And the grey turrets of the castle old
Look'd sternly through the frosty evening-air,   60
Then Iseult took by the hand those children fair,
And brought her tale to an end, and found the path,
And led them home over the darkening heath.

And is she happy? Does she see unmoved
The days in which she might have lived and loved   65
Slip without bringing bliss slowly away,
One after one, to-morrow like to-day?
Joy has not found her yet, nor ever will—
Is it this thought which makes her mien so still,
Her features so fatigued, her eyes, though sweet,   70
So sunk, so rarely lifted save to meet
Her children's? She moves slow; her voice alone
Hath yet an infantine and silver tone,
But even that comes languidly; in truth,
She seems one dying in a mask of youth.   75
And now she will go home, and softly lay
Her laughing children in their beds, and play
Awhile with them before they sleep; and then
She'll light her silver lamp, which fishermen
Dragging their nets through the rough waves, afar,   80
Along this iron coast, know like a star,
And take her broidery-frame, and there she'll sit
Hour after hour, her gold curls sweeping it;

Lifting her soft-bent head only to mind
Her children, or to listen to the wind.   85
And when the clock peals midnight, she will move
Her work away, and let her fingers rove
Across the shaggy brows of Tristram's hound
Who lies, guarding her feet, along the ground;
Or else she will fall musing, her blue eyes   90
Fixt, her slight hands clasp'd on her lap; then rise,
And at her prie-dieu kneel, until she have told
Her rosary-beads of ebony tipp'd with gold,
Then to her soft sleep—and to-morrow'll be
To-day's exact repeated effigy.   95

Yes, it is lonely for her in her hall.
The children, and the grey-hair'd seneschal,
Her women, and Sir Tristram's aged hound,
Are there the sole companions to be found.
But these she loves; and noisier life than this   100
She would find ill to bear, weak as she is.
She has her children, too, and night and day
Is with them; and the wide heaths where they play,
The hollies, and the cliff, and the sea-shore,
The sand, the sea-birds, and the distant sails,   105
These are to her dear as to them; the tales
With which this day the children she beguiled
She gleaned from Breton grandames, when a child,
In every hut along this sea-coast wild.
She herself loves them still, and, when they are told, 110
Can forget all to hear them, as of old.

Dear saints, it is not sorrow, as I hear,
Not suffering, which shuts up eye and ear
To all that has delighted them before,
And lets us be what we were once no more.   115
No, we may suffer deeply, yet retain

Power to be moved and soothed, for all our pain,
By what of old pleased us, and will again.
No, 'tis the gradual furnace of the world,
In whose hot air our spirits are upcurl'd   120
Until they crumble, or else grow like steel—
Which kills in us the bloom, the youth, the spring—
Which leaves the fierce necessity to feel,
But takes away the power—this can avail,
By drying up our joy in everything,   125
To make our former pleasures all seem stale.
This, or some tyrannous single thought, some fit
Of passion, which subdues our souls to it,
Till for its sake alone we live and move—
Call it ambition, or remorse, or love—   130
This too can change us wholly, and make seem
All which we did before, shadow and dream.

  And yet, I swear, it angers me to see
How this fool passion gulls men potently;
Being, in truth, but a diseased unrest,   135
And an unnatural overheat at best.
How they are full of languor and distress
Not having it; which when they do possess,
They straightway are burnt up with fume and care,
And spend their lives in posting here and there   140
Where this plague drives them; and have little ease,
Are furious with themselves, and hard to please.
Like that bald Cæsar, the famed Roman wight,
Who wept at reading of a Grecian knight
Who made a name at younger years than he;   145
Or that renown'd mirror of chivalry,
Prince Alexander, Philip's peerless son,
Who carried the great war from Macedon
Into the Soudan's realm, and thundered on
To die at thirty-five in Babylon.   150

What tale did Iseult to the children say,
Under the hollies, that bright winter's day?

She told them of the fairy-haunted land
Away the other side of Brittany,
Beyond the heaths, edged by the lonely sea;   155
Of the deep forest-glades of Broce-liande,
Through whose green boughs the golden sunshine creeps,
Where Merlin by the enchanted thorn-tree sleeps.
For here he came with the fay Vivian,
One April, when the warm days first began.   160
He was on foot, and that false fay, his friend,
On her white palfrey; here he met his end,
In these lone sylvan glades, that April-day.
This tale of Merlin and the lovely fay
Was the one Iseult chose, and she brought clear   165
Before the children's fancy him and her.

Blowing between the stems, the forest-air
Had loosen'd the brown locks of Vivian's hair,
Which play'd on her flush'd cheek, and her blue eyes
Sparkled with mocking glee and exercise.   170
Her palfrey's flanks were mired and bathed in sweat,
For they had travell'd far and not stopp'd yet.
A brier in that tangled wilderness
Had scored her white right hand, which she allows
To rest ungloved on her green riding-dress;   175
The other warded off the drooping boughs.
But still she chatted on, with her blue eyes
Fix'd full on Merlin's face, her stately prize.
Her 'haviour had the morning's fresh clear grace,
The spirit of the woods was in her face.   180
She look'd so witching fair, that learned wight
Forgot his craft, and his best wits took flight;
And he grew fond, and eager to obey
His mistress, use her empire as she may.

They came to where the brushwood ceased, and day   185
Peer'd 'twixt the stems; and the ground broke away
In a sloped sward down to a brawling brook;
And up as high as where they stood to look
On the brook's farther side was clear, but then
The underwood and trees began again.   190
This open glen was studded thick with thorns
Then white with blossom; and you saw the horns,
Through last year's fern, of the shy fallow-deer
Who come at noon down to the water here.
You saw the bright-eyed squirrels dart along   195
Under the thorns on the green sward; and strong
The blackbird whistled from the dingles near,
And the weird chipping of the woodpecker
Rang lonelily and sharp; the sky was fair,
And a fresh breath of spring stirr'd everywhere.   200
Merlin and Vivian stopp'd on the slope's brow,
To gaze on the light sea of leaf and bough
Which glistering plays all round them, lone and mild,
As if to itself the quiet forest smiled.
Upon the brow-top grew a thorn, and here   205
The grass was dry and moss'd, and you saw clear
Across the hollow; white anemonies
Starr'd the cool turf, and clumps of primroses
Ran out from the dark underwood behind.
No fairer resting-place a man could find.   210
'Here let us halt,' said Merlin then; and she
Nodded, and tied her palfrey to a tree.

They sate them down together, and a sleep
Fell upon Merlin, more like death, so deep.
Her finger on her lips, then Vivian rose,   215
And from her brown-lock'd head the wimple throws,
And takes it in her hand, and waves it over
The blossom'd thorn-tree and her sleeping lover.

Nine times she waved the fluttering wimple round,
And made a little plot of magic ground.   220
And in that daised circle, as men say,
Is Merlin prisoner till the judgment-day;
But she herself whither she will can rove—
For she was passing weary of his love.

A SUMMER NIGHT

Empedocles on Etna (1852)

In the deserted, moon-blanch'd street,
How lonely rings the echo of my feet!
Those windows, which I gaze at, frown,
Silent and white, unopening down,
Repellent as the world;—but see,   5
A break between the housetops shows
The moon! and, lost behind her, fading dim
Into the dewy dark obscurity
Down at the far horizon's rim,
Doth a whole tract of heaven disclose!   10

And to my mind the thought
Is on a sudden brought
Of a past night, and a far different scene.
Headlands stood out into the moonlit deep
As clearly as at noon;   15
The spring-tide's brimming flow
Heaved dazzlingly between;
Houses, with long white sweep,
Girdled the glistening bay;
Behind, through the soft air,   20
The blue haze-cradled mountains spread away,
The night was far more fair—

But the same restless pacings to and fro,
And the same vainly throbbing heart was there,
And the same bright, calm moon.   25

And the calm moonlight seems to say:
Hast thou then still the old unquiet breast,
Which neither deadens into rest,
Nor ever feels the fiery glow
That whirls the spirit from itself away,   30
But fluctuates to and fro,
Never by passion quite possess'd
And never quite benumb'd by the world's sway?—
And I, I know not if to pray
Still to be what I am, or yield and be   35
Like all the other men I see.

For most men in a brazen prison live,
Where, in the sun's hot eye,
With heads bent o'er their toil, they languidly
Their lives to some unmeaning taskwork give,   40
Dreaming of nought beyond their prison-wall.
And as, year after year,
Fresh products of their barren labour fall
From their tired hands, and rest
Never yet comes more near,   45
Gloom settles slowly down over their breast;
And while they try to stem
The waves of mournful thought by which they are prest,
Death in their prison reaches them,
Unfreed, having seen nothing, still unblest.   50

And the rest, a few,
Escape their prison and depart
On the wide ocean of life anew.
There the freed prisoner, where'er his heart

Listeth, will sail;   55
Nor doth he know how there prevail,
Despotic on that sea,
Trade-winds which cross it from eternity.
Awhile he holds some false way, undebarr'd
By thwarting signs, and braves   60
The freshening wind and blackening waves.
And then the tempest strikes him; and between
The lightning-bursts is seen
Only a driving wreck,
And the pale master on his spar-strewn deck   65
With anguish'd face and flying hair
Grasping the rudder hard,
Still bent to make some port he knows not where,
Still standing for some false, impossible shore.
And sterner comes the roar   70
Of sea and wind, and through the deepening gloom
Fainter and fainter wreck and helmsman loom,
And he too disappears, and comes no more.

Is there no life, but these alone?
Madman or slave, must man be one?   75

Plainness and clearness without shadow of stain!
Clearness divine!
Ye heavens, whose pure dark regions have no sign
Of languor, though so calm, and, though so great,
Are yet untroubled and unpassionate;   80
Who, though so noble, share in the world's toil,
And, though so task'd, keep free from dust and soil!
I will not say that your mild deeps retain
A tinge, it may be, of their silent pain
Who have long'd deeply once, and long'd in vain—   85
But I will rather say that you remain
A world above man's head, to let him see
How boundless might his soul's horizons be,

How vast, yet of what clear transparency!
How it were good to abide there, and breathe free;   90
How fair a lot to fill
Is left to each man still!

THE YOUTH OF NATURE

Empedocles on Etna (1852)

RAISED are the dripping oars,
Silent the boat! the lake,
Lovely and soft as a dream,
Swims in the sheen of the moon.
The mountains stand at its head   5
Clear in the pure June-night,
But the valleys are flooded with haze.
Rydal and Fairfield are there;
In the shadow Wordsworth lies dead.
So it is, so it will be for aye.   10
Nature is fresh as of old,
Is lovely; a mortal is dead.

The spots which recall him survive,
For he lent a new life to these hills.
The Pillar still broods o'er the fields   15
Which border Ennerdale Lake,
And Egremont sleeps by the sea.
The gleam of The Evening Star
Twinkles on Grasmere no more,
But ruin'd and solemn and grey   20
The sheepfold of Michael survives;
And, far to the south, the heath
Still blows in the Quantock coombs,
By the favourite waters of Ruth.
These survive!—yet not without pain,   25
Pain and dejection to-night,
Can I feel that their poet is gone.

He grew old in an age he condemn'd.
He look'd on the rushing decay
Of the times which had shelter'd his youth;   30
Felt the dissolving throes
Of a social order he loved;
Outlived his brethren, his peers;
And, like the Theban seer,
Died in his enemies' day.   35

Cold bubbled the spring of Tilphusa,
Copais lay bright in the moon,
Helicon glass'd in the lake
Its firs, and afar rose the peaks
Of Parnassus, snowily clear;   40
Thebes was behind him in flames,
And the clang of arms in his ear,
When his awe-struck captors led
The Theban seer to the spring.
Tiresias drank and died.   45
Nor did reviving Thebes
See such a prophet again.

Well may we mourn, when the head
Of a sacred poet lies low
In an age which can rear them no more!   50
The complaining millions of men
Darken in labour and pain;
But he was a priest to us all
Of the wonder and bloom of the world,
Which we saw with his eyes, and were glad.   55
He is dead, and the fruit-bearing day
Of his race is past on the earth;
And darkness returns to our eyes.

For, oh! is it you, is it you,
Moonlight, and shadow, and lake,   60

And mountains, that fill us with joy,
Or the poet who sings you so well?
Is it you, O beauty, O grace,
O charm, O romance, that we feel,
Or the voice which reveals what you are? 65
Are ye, like daylight and sun,
Shared and rejoiced in by all?
Or are ye immersed in the mass
Of matter, and hard to extract,
Or sunk at the core of the world 70
Too deep for the most to discern?
Like stars in the deep of the sky,
Which arise on the glass of the sage,
But are lost when their watcher is gone.

'They are here'—I heard, as men heard 75
In Mysian Ida the voice
Of the Mighty Mother, or Crete,
The murmur of Nature reply—
'Loveliness, magic, and grace,
They are here! they are set in the world, 80
They abide; and the finest of souls
Hath not been thrill'd by them all,
Nor the dullest been dead to them quite.
The poet who sings them may die,
But they are immortal and live, 85
For they are the life of the world.
Will ye not learn it, and know,
When ye mourn that a poet is dead,
That the singer was less than his themes,
Life, and emotion, and I? 90

'More than the singer are these.
Weak is the tremor of pain
That thrills in his mournfullest chord
To that which once ran through his soul.

Cold the elation of joy 95
In his gladdest, airiest song,
To that which of old in his youth
Fill'd him and made him divine.
Hardly his voice at its best
Gives us a sense of the awe, 100
The vastness, the grandeur, the gloom
Of the unlit gulph of himself.

'Ye know not yourselves; and your bards—
The clearest, the best, who have read
Most in themselves—have beheld 105
Less than they left unreveal'd.
Ye express not yourselves;—can you make
With marble, with colour, with word,
What charm'd you in others re-live?
Can thy pencil, O artist! restore 110
The figure, the bloom of thy love,
As she was in her morning of spring?
Canst thou paint the ineffable smile
Of her eyes as they rested on thine?
Can the image of life have the glow, 115
The motion of life itself?

'Yourselves and your fellows ye know not; and me,
The mateless, the one, will ye know?
Will ye scan me, and read me, and tell
Of the thoughts that ferment in my breast, 120
My longing, my sadness, my joy?
Will ye claim for your great ones the gift
To have render'd the gleam of my skies,
To have echoed the moan of my seas,
Utter'd the voice of my hills? 125
When your great ones depart, will ye say:
All things have suffer'd a loss,
Nature is hid in their grave?

'Race after race, man after man,
Have thought that my secret was theirs,   130
Have dream'd that I lived but for them,
That they were my glory and joy.
—They are dust, they are changed, they are gone!
I remain.'

THE YOUTH OF MAN

Empedocles on Etna (1852)

WE, O Nature, depart,
Thou survivest us! this,
This, I know, is the law.
Yes! but more than this,
Thou who seest us die   5
Seest us change while we live;
Seest our dreams, one by one,
Seest our errors depart;
Watchest us, Nature! throughout,
Mild and inscrutably calm.   10

Well for us that we change!
Well for us that the power
Which in our morning-prime
Saw the mistakes of our youth,
Sweet, and forgiving, and good,   15
Sees the contrition of age!

Behold, O Nature, this pair!
See them to-night where they stand,
Not with the halo of youth
Crowning their brows with its light,   20
Not with the sunshine of hope,
Not with the rapture of spring,
Which they had of old, when they stood

Years ago at my side
In this self-same garden, and said: 25
'We are young, and the world is ours;
Man, man is the king of the world!
Fools that these mystics are
Who prate of Nature! for she
Hath neither beauty, nor warmth,   30
Nor life, nor emotion, nor power.
But man has a thousand gifts,
And the generous dreamer invests
The senseless world with them all.
Nature is nothing; her charm   35
Lives in our eyes which can paint,
Lives in our hearts which can feel.'

Thou, O Nature, wast mute,
Mute as of old! days flew,
Days and years; and Time   40
With the ceaseless stroke of his wings
Brush'd off the bloom from their soul.
Clouded and dim grew their eye,
Languid their heart—for youth
Quicken'd its pulses no more.   45
Slowly, within the walls
Of an ever-narrowing world,
They droop'd, they grew blind, they grew old.
Thee and their youth in thee,
Nature! they saw no more.   50

Murmur of living,
Stir of existence,
Soul of the world!
Make, oh, make yourselves felt
To the dying spirit of youth!   55
Come, like the breath of the spring!

Leave not a human soul
To grow old in darkness and pain!
Only the living can feel you,
But leave us not while we live! **60**

Here they stand to-night—
Here, where this grey balustrade
Crowns the still valley; behind
Is the castled house, with its woods,
Which shelter'd their childhood—the sun **65**
On its ivied windows; a scent
From the grey-wall'd gardens, a breath
Of the fragrant stock and the pink,
Perfumes the evening air.
Their children play on the lawns. **70**
They stand and listen; they hear
The children's shouts, and at times,
Faintly, the bark of a dog
From a distant farm in the hills.
Nothing besides! in front **75**
The wide, wide valley outspreads
To the dim horizon, reposed
In the twilight, and bathed in dew,
Corn-field and hamlet and copse
Darkening fast; but a light, **80**
Far off, a glory of day,
Still plays on the city spires;
And there in the dusk by the walls,
With the grey mist marking its course
Through the silent, flowery land, **85**
On, to the plains, to the sea,
Floats the imperial stream.

Well I know what they feel!
They gaze, and the evening wind

Plays on their faces; they gaze—   90
Airs from the Eden of youth
Awake and stir in their soul;
The past returns—they feel
What they are, alas! what they were.
They, not Nature, are changed.   95
Well I know what they feel!

Hush, for tears
Begin to steal to their eyes!
Hush, for fruit
Grows from such sorrow as theirs!   100
And they remember,
With piercing, untold anguish,
The proud boasting of their youth.
And they feel how Nature was fair.
And the mists of delusion,   105
And the scales of habit,
Fall away from their eyes;
And they see, for a moment,
Stretching out, like the desert
In its weary, unprofitable length,   110
Their faded, ignoble lives.

While the locks are yet brown on thy head,
While the soul still looks through thine eyes,
While the heart still pours
The mantling blood to thy cheek,   115
Sink, O youth, in thy soul!
Yearn to the greatness of Nature;
Rally the good in the depths of thyself!

Brimming   с wonder and joy
He spreads out his arms to the light,   5
Rivets his gaze on the banks of the stream.

As what he sees is, so have his thoughts been.
Whether he wakes,
Where the snowy mountainous pass,
Echoing the screams of the eagles,   10
Hems in its gorges the bed
Of the new-born clear-flowing stream;
Whether he first sees light
Where the river in gleaming rings
Sluggishly winds through the plain;   15
Whether in sound of the swallowing sea—
As is the world on the banks,
So is the mind of the man.

    Vainly does each, as he glides,
Fable and dream   20
Of the lands which the river of Time
Had left ere he woke on its breast,
Or shall reach when his eyes have been closed.
Only the tract where he sails
He wots of; only the thoughts,   25
Raised by the objects he passes, are his.

Who can see the green earth any more
As she was by the sources of Time?
Who imagines her fields as they lay

In the sunshine, unworn by the plough?   30
Who thinks as they thought,
The tribes who then roam'd on her breast,
Her vigorous, primitive sons?

What girl
Now reads in her bosom as clear   35
As Rebekah read, when she sate
At eve by the palm-shaded well?
Who guards in her breast
As deep, as pellucid a spring
Of feeling, as tranquil, as sure?   40

   What bard,
At the height of his vision, can deem
Of God, of the world, of the soul,
With a plainness as near,
As flashing as Moses felt   45
When he lay in the night by his flock
On the starlit Arabian waste?
Can rise and obey
The beck of the Spirit like him?

This tract which the river of Time   50
Now flows through with us, is the plain.
Gone is the calm of its earlier shore.
Border'd by cities and hoarse
With a thousand cries is its stream.
And we on its breast, our minds   55
Are confused as the cries which we hear,
Changing and shot as the sights which we see.

And we say that repose has fled
For ever the course of the river of Time.
That cities will crowd to its edge   60
In a blacker, incessanter line;

That the din will be more on its banks,
Denser the trade on its stream,
Flatter the plain where it flows,
Fiercer the sun overhead.   65
That never will those on its breast
See an ennobling sight,
Drink of the feeling of quiet again.

But what was before us we know not,
And we know not what shall succeed.   70

Haply, the river of Time—
As it grows, as the towns on its marge
Fling their wavering lights
On a wider, statelier stream—
May acquire, if not the calm   75
Of its early mountainous shore,
Yet a solemn peace of its own.

And the width of the waters, the hush
Of the grey expanse where he floats,
Freshening its current and spotted with foam   80
As it draws to the Ocean, may strike
Peace to the soul of the man on its breast—
As the pale waste widens around him,
As the banks fade dimmer away,
As the stars come out, and the night-wind   85
Brings up the stream
Murmurs and scents of the infinite sea.

AND the first grey of morning fill'd the east,
And the fog rose out of the Oxus stream.
But all the Tartar camp along the stream
Was hush'd, and still the men were plunged in sleep;
Sohrab alone, he slept not; all night long   5
He had lain wakeful, tossing on his bed;
But when the grey dawn stole into his tent,
He rose, and clad himself, and girt his sword,
And took his horseman's cloak, and left his tent,
And went abroad into the cold wet fog,   10
Through the dim camp to Peran-Wisa's tent.
    Through the black Tartar tents he pass'd, which stood
Clustering like bee-hives on the low flat strand
Of Oxus, where the summer-floods o'erflow
When the sun melts the snows in high Pamere;   15
Through the black tents he pass'd, o'er that low strand,
And to a hillock came, a little back
From the stream's brink—the spot where first a boat,
Crossing the stream in summer, scrapes the land.
The men of former times had crown'd the top   20
With a clay fort; but that was fall'n, and now
The Tartars built there Peran-Wisa's tent,
A dome of laths, and o'er it felts were spread.
And Sohrab came there, and went in, and stood
Upon the thick piled carpets in the tent,   25
And found the old man sleeping on his bed
Of rugs and felts, and near him lay his arms.
And Peran-Wisa heard him, though the step
Was dull'd; for he slept light, an old man's sleep;
And he rose quickly on one arm, and said:—   30

'Who art thou? for it is not yet clear dawn.
Speak! is there news, or any night alarm?'
    But Sohrab came to the bedside, and said:—
'Thou know'st me, Peran-Wisa! it is I.
The sun is not yet risen, and the foe   35
Sleep; but I sleep not; all night long I lie
Tossing and wakeful, and I come to thee.
For so did King Afrasiab bid me seek
Thy counsel, and to heed thee as thy son,
In Samarcand, before the army march'd;   40
And I will tell thee what my heart desires.
Thou know'st if, since from Ader-baijan first
I came among the Tartars and bore arms,
I have still served Afrasiab well, and shown,
At my boy's years, the courage of a man.   45
This too thou know'st, that while I still bear on
The conquering Tartar ensigns through the world,
And beat the Persians back on every field,
I seek one man, one man, and one alone—
Rustum, my father; who I hoped should greet,   50
Should one day greet, upon some well-fought field,
His not unworthy, not inglorious son.
So I long hoped, but him I never find.
Come then, hear now, and grant me what I ask.
Let the two armies rest to-day; but I   55
Will challenge forth the bravest Persian lords
To meet me, man to man; if I prevail,
Rustum will surely hear it; if I fall—
Old man, the dead need no one, claim no kin.
Dim is the rumour of a common fight,   60
Where host meets host, and many names are sunk;
But of a single combat fame speaks clear.'
    He spoke; and Peran-Wisa took the hand
Of the young man in his, and sigh'd, and said:—
    'Oh Sohrab, an unquiet heart is thine!   65

Canst thou not rest among the Tartar chiefs,
And share the battle's common chance with us
Who love thee, but must press for ever first,
In single fight incurring single risk,
To find a father thou hast never seen?   70
That were far best, my son, to stay with us
Unmurmuring; in our tents, while it is war,
And when 'tis truce, then in Afrasiab's towns.
But, if this one desire indeed rules all,
To seek out Rustum—seek him not through fight!   75
Seek him in peace, and carry to his arms,
O Sohrab, carry an unwounded son!
But far hence seek him, for he is not here.
For now it is not as when I was young,
When Rustum was in front of every fray;   80
But now he keeps apart, and sits at home,
In Seistan, with Zal, his father old.
Whether that his own mighty strength at last
Feels the abhorr'd approaches of old age,
Or in some quarrel with the Persian King.   85
There go!—Thou wilt not? Yet my heart forebodes
Danger or death awaits thee on this field.
Fain would I know thee safe and well, though lost
To us; fain therefore send thee hence, in peace
To seek thy father, not seek single fights   90
In vain;—but who can keep the lion's cub
From ravening, and who govern Rustum's son?
Go, I will grant thee what thy heart desires.'

　So said he, and dropp'd Sohrab's hand, and left
His bed, and the warm rugs whereon he lay;   95
And o'er his chilly limbs his woollen coat
He pass'd, and tied his sandals on his feet,
And threw a white cloak round him, and he took
In his right hand a ruler's staff, no sword;
And on his head he set his sheep-skin cap,   100

Black, glossy, curl'd, the fleece of Kara-Kul;
And raised the curtain of his tent, and call'd
His herald to his side, and went abroad.
The sun by this had risen, and clear'd the fog
From the broad Oxus and the glittering sands.   105
And from their tents the Tartar horsemen filed
Into the open plain; so Haman bade—
Haman, who next to Peran-Wisa ruled
The host, and still was in his lusty prime.
From their black tents, long files of horse, they stream'd;
As when some grey November morn the files,   111
In marching order spread, of long-neck'd cranes
Stream over Casbin and the southern slopes
Of Elburz, from the Aralian estuaries,
Or some frore Caspian reed-bed, southward bound   115
For the warm Persian sea-board—so they stream'd.
The Tartars of the Oxus, the King's guard,
First, with black sheep-skin caps and with long spears;
Large men, large steeds; who from Bokhara come
And Khiva, and ferment the milk of mares.   120
Next, the more temperate Toorkmuns of the south,
The Tukas, and the lances of Salore,
And those from Attruck and the Caspian sands;
Light men and on light steeds, who only drink
The acrid milk of camels, and their wells.   125
And then a swarm of wandering horse, who came
From far, and a more doubtful service own'd;
The Tartars of Ferghana, from the banks
Of the Jaxartes, men with scanty beards
And close-set skull-caps; and those wilder hordes   130
Who roam o'er Kipchak and the northern waste,
Kalmucks and unkempt Kuzzaks, tribes who stray
Nearest the Pole, and wandering Kirghizzes,
Who come on shaggy ponies from Pamere;
These all filed out from camp into the plain.   135

And on the other side the Persians form'd;—
First a light cloud of horse, Tartars they seem'd,
The Ilyats of Khorassan; and behind,
The royal troops of Persia, horse and foot,
Marshall'd battalions bright in burnish'd steel.   140
But Peran-Wisa with his herald came,
Threading the Tartar squadrons to the front,
And with his staff kept back the foremost ranks.
And when Ferood, who led the Persians, saw
That Peran-Wisa kept the Tartars back,   145
He took his spear, and to the front he came,
And check'd his ranks, and fix'd them where they stood.
And the old Tartar came upon the sand
Betwixt the silent hosts, and spake, and said:—
'Ferood, and ye, Persians and Tartars, hear!   150
Let there be truce between the hosts to-day.
But choose a champion from the Persian lords
To fight our champion Sohrab, man to man.'

As, in the country, on a morn in June,
When the dew glistens on the pearled ears,   155
A shiver runs through the deep corn for joy—
So, when they heard what Peran-Wisa said,
A thrill through all the Tartar squadrons ran
Of pride and hope for Sohrab, whom they loved.

But as a troop of pedlars, from Cabool,   160
Cross underneath the Indian Caucasus,
The vast sky-neighbouring mountain of milk snow;
Crossing so high, that, as they mount, they pass
Long flocks of travelling birds dead on the snow,
Choked by the air, and scarce can they themselves   165
Slake their parch'd throats with sugar'd mulberries—
In single file they move, and stop their breath,
For fear they should dislodge the o'erhanging snows—
So the pale Persians held their breath with fear.

And to Ferood his brother chiefs came up   170

To counsel; Gudurz and Zoarrah came,
And Feraburz, who ruled the Persian host
Second, and was the uncle of the King;
These came and counsell'd, and then Gudurz said:—
'Ferood, shame bids us take their challenge up,   175
Yet champion have we none to match this youth.
He has the wild stag's foot, the lion's heart.
But Rustum came last night; aloof he sits
And sullen, and has pitch'd his tents apart.
Him will I seek, and carry to his ear   180
The Tartar challenge, and this young man's name.
Haply he will forget his wrath, and fight.
Stand forth the while, and take their challenge up.'
So spake he; and Ferood stood forth and cried:—
'Old man, be it agreed as thou hast said!   185
Let Sohrab arm, and we will find a man.'
He spake: and Peran-Wisa turn'd, and strode
Back through the opening squadrons to his tent.
But through the anxious Persians Gudurz ran,
And cross'd the camp which lay behind, and reach'd,   190
Out on the sands beyond it, Rustum's tents.
Of scarlet cloth they were, and glittering gay,
Just pitch'd; the high pavilion in the midst
Was Rustum's, and his men lay camp'd around.
And Gudurz enter'd Rustum's tent, and found   195
Rustum; his morning meal was done, but still
The table stood before him, charged with food—
A side of roasted sheep, and cakes of bread,
And dark green melons; and there Rustum sate
Listless, and held a falcon on his wrist,   200
And play'd with it; but Gudurz came and stood
Before him; and he look'd, and saw him stand,
And with a cry sprang up and dropp'd the bird,
And greeted Gudurz with both hands, and said:—
'Welcome! these eyes could see no better sight.   205

What news? but sit down first, and eat and drink.'
  But Gudurz stood in the tent-door, and said:—
'Not now! a time will come to eat and drink,
But not to-day; to-day has other needs.
The armies are drawn out, and stand at gaze;   210
For from the Tartars is a challenge brought
To pick a champion from the Persian lords
To fight their champion—and thou know'st his name—
Sohrab men call him, but his birth is hid.
O Rustum, like thy might is this young man's!   215
He has the wild stag's foot, the lion's heart;
And he is young, and Iran's chiefs are old,
Or else too weak; and all eyes turn to thee.
Come down and help us, Rustum, or we lose!'
  He spoke; but Rustum answer'd with a smile:—   220
'Go to! if Iran's chiefs are old, then I
Am older; if the young are weak, the King
Errs strangely; for the King, for Kai Khosroo,
Himself is young, and honours younger men,
And lets the aged moulder to their graves.   225
Rustum he loves no more, but loves the young—
The young may rise at Sohrab's vaunts, not I.
For what care I, though all speak Sohrab's fame?
For would that I myself had such a son,
And not that one slight helpless girl I have—   230
A son so famed, so brave, to send to war,
And I to tarry with the snow-hair'd Zal,
My father, whom the robber Afghans vex,
And clip his borders short, and drive his herds,
And he has none to guard his weak old age.   235
There would I go, and hang my armour up,
And with my great name fence that weak old man,
And spend the goodly treasures I have got,
And rest my age, and hear of Sohrab's fame,
And leave to death the hosts of thankless kings,   240

And with these slaughterous hands draw sword no more.'
He spoke, and smiled; and Gudurz made reply:—
'What then, O Rustum, will men say to this,
When Sohrab dares our bravest forth, and seeks
Thee most of all, and thou, whom most he seeks,   245
Hidest thy face? Take heed lest men should say:
Like some old miser, Rustum hoards his fame,
And shuns to peril it with younger men.'
And, greatly moved, then Rustum made reply:—
'O Gudurz, wherefore dost thou say such words?   250
Thou knowest better words than this to say.
What is one more, one less, obscure or famed,
Valiant or craven, young or old, to me?
Are not they mortal, am not I myself?
But who for men of nought would do great deeds?   255
Come, thou shalt see how Rustum hoards his fame!
But I will fight unknown, and in plain arms;
Let not men say of Rustum, he was match'd
In single fight with any mortal man.'
He spoke, and frown'd; and Gudurz turn'd, and ran 260
Back quickly through the camp in fear and joy—
Fear at his wrath, but joy that Rustum came.
But Rustum strode to his tent-door, and call'd
His followers in, and bade them bring his arms,
And clad himself in steel; the arms he chose   265
Were plain, and on his shield was no device,
Only his helm was rich, inlaid with gold,
And, from the fluted spine atop, a plume
Of horsehair waved, a scarlet horsehair plume.
So arm'd, he issued forth; and Ruksh, his horse,   270
Follow'd him like a faithful hound at heel—
Ruksh, whose renown was noised through all the earth,
The horse, whom Rustum on a foray once
Did in Bokhara by the river find
A colt beneath its dam, and drove him home,   275

And rear'd him; a bright bay, with lofty crest,
Dight with a saddle-cloth of broider'd green
Crusted with gold, and on the ground were work'd
All beasts of chase, all beasts which hunters know.
So follow'd, Rustum left his tents, and cross'd   280
The camp, and to the Persian host appear'd.
And all the Persians knew him, and with shouts
Hail'd; but the Tartars knew not who he was.
And dear as the wet diver to the eyes
Of his pale wife who waits and weeps on shore,   285
By sandy Bahrein, in the Persian Gulf,
Plunging all day in the blue waves, at night,
Having made up his tale of precious pearls,
Rejoins her in their hut upon the sands—
So dear to the pale Persians Rustum came.   290
   And Rustum to the Persian front advanced,
And Sohrab arm'd in Haman's tent, and came.
And as afield the reapers cut a swath
Down through the middle of a rich man's corn,
And on each side are squares of standing corn,   295
And in the midst a stubble, short and bare—
So on each side were squares of men, with spears
Bristling, and in the midst, the open sand.
And Rustum came upon the sand, and cast
His eyes toward the Tartar tents, and saw   300
Sohrab come forth, and eyed him as he came.
   As some rich woman, on a winter's morn,
Eyes through her silken curtains the poor drudge
Who with numb blacken'd fingers makes her fire—
At cock-crow, on a starlit winter's morn,   305
When the frost flowers the whiten'd window-panes—
And wonders how she lives, and what the thoughts
Of that poor drudge may be; so Rustum eyed
The unknown adventurous youth, who from afar
Came seeking Rustum, and defying forth   310

All the most valiant chiefs; long he perused
His spirited air, and wonder'd who he was.
For very young he seem'd, tenderly rear'd;
Like some young cypress, tall, and dark, and straight,
Which in a queen's secluded garden throws   315
Its slight dark shadow on the moonlit turf,
By midnight, to a bubbling fountain's sound—
So slender Sohrab seem'd, so softly rear'd.
And a deep pity enter'd Rustum's soul
As he beheld him coming; and he stood,   320
And beckon'd to him with his hand, and said:—
   'O thou young man, the air of Heaven is soft,
And warm, and pleasant; but the grave is cold!
Heaven's air is better than the cold dead grave.
Behold me! I am vast, and clad in iron,   325
And tried; and I have stood on many a field
Of blood, and I have fought with many a foe—
Never was that field lost, or that foe saved.
O Sohrab, wherefore wilt thou rush on death?
Be govern'd! quit the Tartar host, and come   330
To Iran, and be as my son to me,
And fight beneath my banner till I die!
There are no youths in Iran brave as thou.'
   So he spake, mildly; Sohrab heard his voice,
The mighty voice of Rustum, and he saw   335
His giant figure planted on the sand,
Sole, like some single tower, which a chief
Hath builded on the waste in former years
Against the robbers; and he saw that head,
Streak'd with its first grey hairs;—hope filled his soul, 340
And he ran forward and embraced his knees,
And clasp'd his hand within his own, and said:—
   'O, by thy father's head! by thine own soul!
Art thou not Rustum? speak! art thou not he?'
   But Rustum eyed askance the kneeling youth,   345

And turn'd away, and spake to his own soul:—
    'Ah me, I muse what this young fox may mean!
False, wily, boastful, are these Tartar boys.
For if I now confess this thing he asks,
And hide it not, but say: *Rustum is here!*   350
He will not yield indeed, nor quit our foes,
But he will find some pretext not to fight,
And praise my fame, and proffer courteous gifts,
A belt or sword perhaps, and go his way.
And on a feast-tide, in Afrasiab's hall,   355
In Samarcand, he will arise and cry:
"I challenged once, when the two armies camp'd
Beside the Oxus, all the Persian lords
To cope with me in single fight; but they
Shrank, only Rustum dared; then he and I   360
Changed gifts, and went on equal terms away."
So will he speak, perhaps, while men applaud;
Then were the chiefs of Iran shamed through me.'
    And then he turned, and sternly spake aloud:—
'Rise! wherefore dost thou vainly question thus   365
Of Rustum? I am here, whom thou hast call'd
By challenge forth; make good thy vaunt, or yield!
Is it with Rustum only thou wouldst fight?
Rash boy, men look on Rustum's face and flee!
For well I know, that did great Rustum stand   370
Before thy face this day, and were reveal'd,
There would be then no talk of fighting more.
But being what I am, I tell thee this—
Do thou record it in thine inmost soul:
Either thou shalt renounce thy vaunt and yield,   375
Or else thy bones shall strew this sand, till winds
Bleach them, or Oxus with his summer-floods,
Oxus in summer wash them all away.'
    He spoke; and Sohrab answer'd, on his feet:—
'Art thou so fierce? Thou wilt not fright me so!   380

I am no girl, to be made pale by words.
Yet this thou hast said well, did Rustum stand
Here on this field, there were no fighting then.
But Rustum is far hence, and we stand here.
Begin! thou art more vast, more dread than I,　　　385
And thou art proved, I know, and I am young—
But yet success sways with the breath of Heaven.
And though thou thinkest that thou knowest sure
Thy victory, yet thou canst not surely know.
For we are all, like swimmers in the sea,　　　390
Poised on the top of a huge wave of fate,
Which hangs uncertain to which side to fall.
And whether it will heave us up to land,
Or whether it will roll us out to sea,
Back out to sea, to the deep waves of death,　　　395
We know not, and no search will make us know;
Only the event will teach us in its hour.'
　　He spoke, and Rustum answer'd not, but hurl'd
His spear; down from the shoulder, down it came,
As on some partridge in the corn a hawk,　　　400
That long has tower'd in the airy clouds,
Drops like a plummet; Sohrab saw it come,
And sprang aside, quick as a flash; the spear
Hiss'd, and went quivering down into the sand,
Which it sent flying wide;—then Sohrab threw　　　405
In turn, and full struck Rustum's shield; sharp rang,
The iron plates rang sharp, but turn'd the spear.
And Rustum seized his club, which none but he
Could wield; an unlopp'd trunk it was, and huge,
Still rough—like those which men in treeless plains　　　410
To build them boats fish from the flooded rivers,
Hyphasis or Hydaspes, when, high up
By their dark springs, the wind in winter-time
Hath made in Himalayan forests wrack,
And strewn the channels with torn boughs—so huge　　　415

The club which Rustum lifted now, and struck
One stroke; but again Sohrab sprang aside,
Lithe as the glancing snake, and the club came
Thundering to earth, and leapt from Rustum's hand.
And Rustum follow'd his own blow, and fell   420
To his knees, and with his fingers clutch'd the sand;
And now might Sohrab have unsheathed his sword,
And pierced the mighty Rustum while he lay
Dizzy, and on his knees, and choked with sand;
But he look'd on, and smiled, nor bared his sword, 425
But courteously drew back, and spoke, and said:—
   'Thou strik'st too hard! that club of thine will float
Upon the summer-floods, and not my bones.
But rise, and be not wroth! not wroth am I;
No, when I see thee, wrath forsakes my soul.   430
Thou say'st, thou art not Rustum; be it so!
Who art thou then, that canst so touch my soul?
Boy as I am, I have seen battles too—
Have waded foremost in their bloody waves,
And heard their hollow roar of dying men;   435
But never was my heart thus touch'd before.
Are they from Heaven, these softenings of the heart?
O thou old warrior, let us yield to Heaven!
Come, plant we here in earth our angry spears,
And make a truce, and sit upon this sand,   440
And pledge each other in red wine, like friends,
And thou shalt talk to me of Rustum's deeds.
There are enough foes in the Persian host,
Whom I may meet, and strike, and feel no pang;
Champions enough Afrasiab has, whom thou   445
Mayst fight; fight *them*, when they confront thy spear!
But oh, let there be peace 'twixt thee and me!'
   He ceased, but while he spake, Rustum had risen,
And stood erect, trembling with rage; his club
He left to lie, but had regain'd his spear,   450

Whose fiery point now in his mail'd right-hand
Blazed bright and baleful, like that autumn-star,
The baleful sign of fevers; dust had soil'd
His stately crest, and dimm'd his glittering arms.
His breast heaved, his lips foam'd, and twice his voice   455
Was choked with rage; at last these words broke way:—
　'Girl! nimble with thy feet, not with thy hands!
Curl'd minion, dancer, coiner of sweet words!
Fight, let me hear thy hateful voice no more!
Thou art not in Afrasiab's gardens now   460
With Tartar girls, with whom thou art wont to dance;
But on the Oxus-sands, and in the dance
Of battle, and with me, who make no play
Of war; I fight it out, and hand to hand.
Speak not to me of truce, and pledge, and wine!   465
Remember all thy valour; try thy feints
And cunning! all the pity I had is gone;
Because thou hast shamed me before both the hosts
With thy light skipping tricks, and thy girl's wiles.'
　He spoke, and Sohrab kindled at his taunts,   470
And he too drew his sword; at once they rush'd
Together, as two eagles on one prey
Come rushing down together from the clouds,
One from the east, one from the west; their shields
Dash'd with a clang together, and a din   475
Rose, such as that the sinewy woodcutters
Make often in the forest's heart at morn,
Of hewing axes, crashing trees—such blows
Rustum and Sohrab on each other hail'd.
And you would say that sun and stars took part   480
In that unnatural conflict; for a cloud
Grew suddenly in Heaven, and dark'd the sun
Over the fighters' heads; and a wind rose
Under their feet, and moaning swept the plain,
And in a sandy whirlwind wrapp'd the pair.   485

In gloom they twain were wrapp'd, and they alone;
For both the on-looking hosts on either hand
Stood in broad daylight, and the sky was pure,
And the sun sparkled on the Oxus stream.
But in the gloom they fought, with bloodshot eyes   490
And labouring breath; first Rustum struck the shield
Which Sohrab held stiff out; the steel-spiked spear
Rent the tough plates, but fail'd to reach the skin,
And Rustum pluck'd it back with angry groan.
Then Sohrab with his sword smote Rustum's helm,   495
Nor clove its steel quite through; but all the crest
He shore away, and that proud horsehair plume,
Never till now defiled, sank to the dust;
And Rustum bow'd his head; but then the gloom
Grew blacker, thunder rumbled in the air,   500
And lightnings rent the cloud; and Ruksh, the horse,
Who stood at hand, utter'd a dreadful cry;—
No horse's cry was that, most like the roar
Of some pain'd desert-lion, who all day
Hath trail'd the hunter's javelin in his side,   505
And comes at night to die upon the sand.
The two hosts heard that cry, and quaked for fear,
And Oxus curdled as it cross'd his stream.
But Sohrab heard, and quail'd not, but rush'd on,
And struck again; and again Rustum bow'd   510
His head; but this time all the blade, like glass,
Sprang in a thousand shivers on the helm,
And in the hand the hilt remain'd alone.
Then Rustum raised his head; his dreadful eyes
Glared, and he shook on high his menacing spear,   515
And shouted: *Rustum!*—Sohrab heard that shout,
And shrank amazed; back he recoil'd one step,
And scann'd with blinking eyes the advancing form;
And then he stood bewilder'd; and he dropp'd
His covering shield, and the spear pierced his side.   520

He reel'd, and staggering back, sank to the ground;
And then the gloom dispersed, and the wind fell,
And the bright sun broke forth, and melted all
The cloud; and the two armies saw the pair—
Saw Rustum standing, safe upon his feet,   525
And Sohrab, wounded, on the bloody sand.

    Then, with a bitter smile, Rustum began:—
'Sohrab, thou thoughtest in thy mind to kill
A Persian lord this day, and strip his corpse,
And bear thy trophies to Afrasiab's tent.   530
Or else that the great Rustum would come down
Himself to fight, and that thy wiles would move
His heart to take a gift, and let thee go.
And then that all the Tartar host would praise
Thy courage or thy craft, and spread thy fame,   535
To glad thy father in his weak old age.
Fool, thou art slain, and by an unknown man!
Dearer to the red jackals shalt thou be
Than to thy friends, and to thy father old.'

    And, with a fearless mien, Sohrab replied:—   540
'Unknown thou art; yet thy fierce vaunt is vain.
Thou dost not slay me, proud and boastful man!
No! Rustum slays me, and this filial heart.
For were I match'd with ten such men as thee,
And I were that which till to-day I was,   545
They should be lying here, I standing there.
But that belovéd name unnerved my arm—
That name, and something, I confess, in thee,
Which troubles all my heart, and made my shield
Fall; and thy spear transfix'd an unarm'd foe.   550
And now thou boastest, and insult'st my fate.
But hear thou this, fierce man, tremble to hear:
The mighty Rustum shall avenge my death!
My father, whom I seek through all the world,
He shall avenge my death, and punish thee!'   555

As when some hunter in the spring hath found
A breeding eagle sitting on her nest,
Upon the craggy isle of a hill-lake,
And pierced her with an arrow as she rose,
And follow'd her to find her where she fell   560
Far off;—anon her mate comes winging back
From hunting, and a great way off descries
His huddling young left sole; at that, he checks
His pinion, and with short uneasy sweeps
Circles above his eyry, with loud screams   565
Chiding his mate back to her nest; but she
Lies dying, with the arrow in her side,
In some far stony gorge out of his ken,
A heap of fluttering feathers—never more
Shall the lake glass her, flying over it;   570
Never the black and dripping precipices
Echo her stormy scream as she sails by—
As that poor bird flies home, nor knows his loss,
So Rustum knew not his own loss, but stood
Over his dying son, and knew him not.   575
    But, with a cold incredulous voice, he said:—
'What prate is this of fathers and revenge?
The mighty Rustum never had a son.'
    And, with a failing voice, Sohrab replied:—
'Ah yes, he had! and that lost son am I.   580
Surely the news will one day reach his ear,
Reach Rustum, where he sits, and tarries long,
Somewhere, I know not where, but far from here;
And pierce him like a stab, and make him leap
To arms, and cry for vengeance upon thee.   585
Fierce man, bethink thee, for an only son!
What will that grief, what will that vengeance be?
Oh, could I live, till I that grief had seen!
Yet him I pity not so much, but her,
My mother, who in Ader-baijan dwells   590

With that old king, her father, who grows grey
With age, and rules over the valiant Koords.
Her most I pity, who no more will see
Sohrab returning from the Tartar camp,
With spoils and honour, when the war is done.   595
But a dark rumour will be bruited up,
From tribe to tribe, until it reach her ear;
And then will that defenceless woman learn
That Sohrab will rejoice her sight no more,
But that in battle with a nameless foe,   600
By the far-distant Oxus, he is slain.'

  He spoke; and as he ceased, he wept aloud,
Thinking of her he left, and his own death.
He spoke; but Rustum listen'd, plunged in thought.
Nor did he yet believe it was his son   605
Who spoke, although he call'd back names he knew;
For he had had sure tidings that the babe,
Which was in Ader-baijan born to him,
Had been a puny girl, no boy at all—
So that sad mother sent him word, for fear   610
Rustum should seek the boy, to train in arms;
And so he deem'd that either Sohrab took,
By a false boast, the style of Rustum's son;
Or that men gave it him, to swell his fame.
So deem'd he; yet he listen'd, plunged in thought   615
And his soul set to grief, as the vast tide
Of the bright rocking Ocean sets to shore
At the full moon; tears gather'd in his eyes;
For he remember'd his own early youth,
And all its bounding rapture; as, at dawn,   620
The shepherd from his mountain lodge descries
A far, bright city, smitten by the sun,
Through many rolling clouds—so Rustum saw
His youth; saw Sohrab's mother, in her bloom;
And that old king, her father, who loved well   625

His wandering guest, and gave him his fair child
With joy; and all the pleasant life they led,
They three, in that long-distant summer-time—
The castle, and the dewy woods, and hunt
And hound, and morn on those delightful hills　　630
In Ader-baijan. And he saw that Youth,
Of age and looks to be his own dear son,
Piteous and lovely, lying on the sand,
Like some rich hyacinth which by the scythe
Of an unskilful gardener has been cut,　　635
Mowing the garden grass-plots near its bed,
And lies, a fragrant tower of purple bloom,
On the mown, dying grass—so Sohrab lay,
Lovely in death, upon the common sand.
And Rustum gazed on him with grief, and said:—　　640
　'O Sohrab, thou indeed art such a son
Whom Rustum, wert thou his, might well have loved.
Yet here thou errest, Sohrab, or else men
Have told thee false—thou art not Rustum's son.
For Rustum had no son; one child he had—　　645
But one—a girl; who with her mother now
Plies some light female task, nor dreams of us—
Of us she dreams not, nor of wounds, nor war.'
　But Sohrab answer'd him in wrath; for now
The anguish of the deep-fix'd spear grew fierce,　　650
And he desired to draw forth the steel,
And let the blood flow free, and so to die—
But first he would convince his stubborn foe;
And, rising sternly on one arm, he said:—
　'Man, who art thou who dost deny my words?　　655
Truth sits upon the lips of dying men,
And falsehood, while I lived, was far from mine.
I tell thee, prick'd upon this arm I bear
That seal which Rustum to my mother gave,
That she might prick it on the babe she bore.'　　660

He spoke; and all the blood left Rustum's cheeks,
And his knees totter'd, and he smote his hand
Against his breast, his heavy mailed hand,
That the hard iron corslet clank'd aloud;
And to his heart he press'd the other hand,   665
And in a hollow voice he spake, and said:—
  'Sohrab, that were a proof which could not lie!
If thou show this, then art thou Rustum's son.'
  Then, with weak hasty fingers, Sohrab loosed
His belt, and near the shoulder bared his arm,   670
And show'd a sign in faint vermilion points
Prick'd; as a cunning workman, in Pekin,
Pricks with vermilion some clear porcelain vase,
An emperor's gift—at early morn he paints,
And all day long, and, when night comes, the lamp   675
Lights up his studious forehead and thin hands—
So delicately prick'd the sign appear'd
On Sohrab's arm, the sign of Rustum's seal.
It was that griffin, which of old rear'd Zal,
Rustum's great father, whom they left to die,   680
A helpless babe, among the mountain-rocks;
Him that kind creature found, and rear'd, and loved—
Then Rustum took it for his glorious sign.
And Sohrab bared that image on his arm,
And himself scann'd it long with mournful eyes,   685
And then he touch'd it with his hand and said:—
  'How say'st thou? Is that sign the proper sign
Of Rustum's son, or of some other man's?'
  He spoke; but Rustum gazed, and gazed, and stood
Speechless; and then he utter'd one sharp cry: 690
O boy—thy father!—and his voice choked there.
And then a dark cloud pass'd before his eyes,
And his head swam, and he sank down to earth.
But Sohrab crawl'd to where he lay, and cast
His arms about his neck, and kiss'd his lips,   695

And with fond faltering fingers stroked his cheeks,
Trying to call him back to life; and life
Came back to Rustum, and he oped his eyes,
And they stood wide with horror; and he seized
In both his hands the dust which lay around,   700
And threw it on his head, and smirch'd his hair,—
His hair, and face, and beard, and glittering arms;
And strong convulsive groanings shook his breast,
And his sobs choked him; and he clutch'd his sword,
To draw it, and for ever let life out.   705
But Sohrab saw his thought, and held his hands,
And with a soothing voice he spake, and said:—

  'Father, forbear! for I but meet to-day
The doom which at my birth was written down
In Heaven, and thou art Heaven's unconscious hand.   710
Surely my heart cried out that it was thou,
When first I saw thee; and thy heart spoke too,
I know it! but fate trod those promptings down
Under its iron heel; fate, fate engaged
The strife, and hurl'd me on my father's spear.   715
But let us speak no more of this! I find
My father; let me feel that I have found!
Come, sit beside me on this sand, and take
My head betwixt thy hands, and kiss my cheeks,
And wash them with thy tears, and say: *My son!*   720
Quick! quick! for number'd are my sands of life,
And swift; for like the lightning to this field
I came, and like the wind I go away—
Sudden, and swift, and like a passing wind.
But it was writ in Heaven that this should be.'   725
  So said he, and his voice released the heart
Of Rustum, and his tears broke forth; he cast
His arms round his son's neck, and wept aloud,
And kiss'd him. And awe fell on both the hosts,
When they saw Rustum's grief; and Ruksh, the horse,   730

With his head bowing to the ground and mane
Sweeping the dust, came near, and in mute woe
First to the one then to the other moved
His head, as if inquiring what their grief
Might mean; and from his dark, compassionate eyes,   735
The big warm tears roll'd down, and caked the sand.
But Rustum chid him with stern voice, and said:—
  'Ruksh, now thou grievest; but, O Ruksh, thy feet
Should first have rotted on their nimble joints,
Or ere they brought thy master to this field!'   740
  But Sohrab look'd upon the horse and said;—
'Is this, then, Ruksh? How often, in past days,
My mother told me of thee, thou brave steed,
My terrible father's terrible horse! and said,
That I should one day find thy lord and thee.   745
Come, let me lay my hand upon thy mane!
O Ruksh, thou art more fortunate than I;
For thou hast gone where I shall never go,
And snuff'd the breezes of my father's home.
And thou hast trod the sands of Seistan,   750
And seen the River of Helmund, and the Lake
Of Zirrah; and the aged Zal himself
Has often stroked thy neck, and given thee food,
Corn in a golden platter soak'd with wine,
And said; *O Ruksh! bear Rustum well!*—but I   755
Have never known my grandsire's furrow'd face,
Nor seen his lofty house in Seistan,
Nor slaked my thirst at the clear Helmund stream;
But lodged among my father's foes, and seen
Afrasiab's cities only, Samarcand,   760
Bokhara, and lone Khiva in the waste,
And the black Toorkmun tents; and only drunk
The desert rivers, Moorghab and Tejend,
Kohik, and where the Kalmuks feed their sheep,
The northern Sir; and this great Oxus stream,   765

The yellow Oxus, by whose brink I die.'
   Then, with a heavy groan, Rustum bewail'd:—
'Oh, that its waves were flowing over me!
Oh, that I saw its grains of yellow silt
Roll tumbling in the current o'er my head!'   770
   But, with a grave mild voice, Sohrab replied:—
'Desire not that, my father! thou must live.
For some are born to do great deeds, and live,
As some are born to be obscured, and die.
Do thou the deeds I die too young to do,   775
And reap a second glory in thine age;
Thou art my father, and thy gain is mine.
But come! thou seest this great host of men
Which follow me; I pray thee, slay not these!
Let me entreat for them; what have they done?   780
They follow'd me, my hope, my fame, my star.
Let them all cross the Oxus back in peace.
But me thou must bear hence, not send with them,
But carry me with thee to Seistan,
And place me on a bed, and mourn for me,   785
Thou, and the snow-hair'd Zal, and all thy friends.
And thou must lay me in that lovely earth,
And heap a stately mound above my bones,
And plant a far-seen pillar over all.
That so the passing horseman on the waste   790
May see my tomb a great way off, and cry:
Sohrab, the mighty Rustum's son, lies there,
Whom his great father did in ignorance kill!
And I be not forgotten in my grave.'
   And, with a mournful voice, Rustum replied:—   795
'Fear not! as thou hast said, Sohrab, my son,
So shall it be; for I will burn my tents,
And quit the host, and bear thee hence with me,
And carry thee away to Seistan,
And place thee on a bed, and mourn for thee,   800

With the snow-headed Zal, and all my friends.
And I will lay thee in that lovely earth,
And heap a stately mound above thy bones,
And plant a far-seen pillar over all,
And men shall not forget thee in thy grave.   805
And I will spare thy host; yea, let them go!
Let them all cross the Oxus back in peace!
What should I do with slaying any more?
For would that all that I have ever slain
Might be once more alive; my bitterest foes,   810
And they who were call'd champions in their time,
And through whose death I won that fame I have—
And I were nothing but a common man,
A poor, mean soldier, and without renown,
So thou mightest live too, my son, my son!   815
Or rather would that I, even I myself,
Might now be lying on this bloody sand,
Near death, and by an ignorant stroke of thine,
Not thou of mine! and I might die, not thou;
And I, not thou, be borne to Seistan;   820
And Zal might weep above my grave, not thine;
And say: *O son, I weep thee not too sore,*
For willingly, I know, thou met'st thine end!
But now in blood and battles was my youth,
And full of blood and battles is my age,   825
And I shall never end this life of blood.'
   Then, at the point of death, Sohrab replied:—
'A life of blood indeed, thou dreadful man!
But thou shalt yet have peace; only not now,
Not yet! but thou shalt have it on that day,   830
When thou shalt sail in a high-masted ship,
Thou and the other peers of Kai Khosroo,
Returning home over the salt blue sea,
From laying thy dear master in his grave.'
   And Rustum gazed in Sohrab's face, and said:—   835

'Soon be that day, my son, and deep that sea!
Till then, if fate so wills, let me endure.'
He spoke; and Sohrab smiled on him, and took
The spear, and drew it from his side, and eased
His wound's imperious anguish; but the blood   840
Came welling from the open gash, and life
Flow'd with the stream;—all down his cold white side
The crimson torrent ran, dim now and soil'd,
Like the soil'd tissue of white violets
Left, freshly gather'd, on their native bank,   845
By children whom their nurses call with haste
Indoors from the sun's eye; his head droop'd low,
His limbs grew slack; motionless, white, he lay—
White, with eyes closed; only when heavy gasps,
Deep heavy gasps quivering through all his frame,   850
Convulsed him back to life, he open'd them,
And fix'd them feebly on his father's face;
Till now all strength was ebb'd, and from his limbs
Unwillingly the spirit fled away,
Regretting the warm mansion which it left,   855
And youth, and bloom, and this delightful world.
So, on the bloody sand, Sohrab lay dead;
And the great Rustum drew his horseman's cloak
Down o'er his face, and sate by his dead son.
As those black granite pillars, once high-rear'd   860
By Jemshid in Persepolis, to bear
His house, now 'mid their broken flights of steps
Lie prone, enormous, down the mountain side—
So in the sand lay Rustum by his son.
And night came down over the solemn waste,   865
And the two gazing hosts, and that sole pair,
And darken'd all; and a cold fog, with night,
Crept from the Oxus. Soon a hum arose,
As of a great assembly loosed, and fires
Began to twinkle through the fog; for now   870

Both armies moved to camp, and took their meal;
The Persians took it on the open sands
Southward, the Tartars by the river marge;
And Rustum and his son were left alone.

But the majestic river floated on,   875
Out of the mist and hum of that low land,
Into the frosty starlight, and there moved,
Rejoicing, through the hush'd Chorasmian waste,
Under the solitary moon;—he flow'd
Right for the polar star, past Orgunjè,   880
Brimming, and bright, and large; then sands begin
To hem his watery march, and dam his streams,
And split his currents; that for many a league
The shorn and parcell'd Oxus strains along
Through beds of sand and matted rushy isles—   885
Oxus, forgetting the bright speed he had
In his high mountain-cradle in Pamere,
A foil'd circuitous wanderer—till at last
The long'd-for dash of waves is heard, and wide
His luminous home of waters opens, bright   890
And tranquil, from whose floor the new-bathed stars
Emerge, and shine upon the Aral Sea.

THE TOMB IN THE CHURCH OF BROU

Poems (1853)

So rest, for ever rest, O princely Pair!
In your high church, 'mid the still mountain-air,
Where horn, and hound, and vassals, never come.
Only the blessed Saints are smiling dumb,
From the rich painted windows of the nave,   5
On aisle, and transept, and your marble grave;
Where thou, young Prince! shalt never more arise
From the fringed mattress where thy Duchess lies,

On autumn mornings, when the bugle sounds,
And ride across the drawbridge with thy hounds   10
To hunt the boar in the crisp woods till eve;
And thou, O Princess! shalt no more receive,
Thou and thy ladies, in the hall of state,
The jaded hunters with their bloody freight,
Coming benighted to the castle-gate.   15
  So sleep, for ever sleep, O marble Pair!
Or, if ye wake, let it be then, when fair
On the carved western front a flood of light
Streams from the setting sun, and colours bright
Prophets, transfigured Saints, and Martyrs brave,   20
In the vast western window of the nave;
And on the pavement round the Tomb there glints
A chequer-work of glowing sapphire-tints,
And amethyst, and ruby—then unclose
Your eyelids on the stone where ye repose,   25
And from your broider'd pillows lift your heads,
And rise upon your cold white marble beds;
And, looking down on the warm rosy tints,
Which chequer, at your feet, the illumined flints,
Say: *What is this? we are in bliss—forgiven—*   30
Behold the pavement of the courts of Heaven!
Or let it be on autumn nights, when rain
Doth rustlingly above your heads complain
On the smooth leaden roof, and on the walls
Shedding her pensive light at intervals   35
The moon through the clere-story windows shines,
And the wind washes through the mountain-pines.
Then, gazing up 'mid the dim pillars high,
The foliaged marble forest where ye lie,
Hush, ye will say, *it is eternity!*   40
This is the glimmering verge of Heaven, and these
The columns of the heavenly palaces!
And, in the sweeping of the wind, your ear

The passage of the Angels' wings will hear,
And on the lichen-crusted leads above 45
The rustle of the eternal rain of love.

REQUIESCAT

Poems (1853)

STREW on her roses, roses,
 And never a spray of yew!
In quiet she reposes;
 Ah, would that I did too!

Her mirth the world required; 5
 She bathed it in smiles of glee.
But her heart was tired, tired,
 And now they let her be.

Her life was turning, turning,
 In mazes of heat and sound. 10
But for peace her soul was yearning,
 And now peace laps her round.

Her cabin'd, ample spirit,
 It flutter'd and fail'd for breath.
To-night it doth inherit 15
 The vasty hall of death.

THE SCHOLAR-GIPSY

Poems (1853)

GO, for they call you, shepherd, from the hill;
 Go, shepherd, and untie the wattled cotes!
  No longer leave thy wistful flock unfed,
 Nor let thy bawling fellows rack their throats,
 Nor the cropp'd herbage shoot another head. 5
  But when the fields are still,

And the tired men and dogs all gone to rest,
   And only the white sheep are sometimes seen
   Cross and recross the strips of moon-blanch'd green,
Come, shepherd, and again begin the quest!   10

Here, where the reaper was at work of late—
   In this high field's dark corner, where he leaves
   His coat, his basket, and his earthen cruse,
   And in the sun all morning binds the sheaves,
     Then here, at noon, comes back his stores to use—   15
      Here will I sit and wait,
   While to my ear from uplands far away
   The bleating of the folded flocks is borne,
   With distant cries of reapers in the corn—
All the live murmur of a summer's day.   20

Screen'd is this nook o'er the high, half-reap'd field,
   And here till sun-down, shepherd! will I be.
     Through the thick corn the scarlet poppies peep.
   And round green roots and yellowing stalks I see
     Pale pink convolvulus in tendrils creep;   25
      And air-swept lindens yield
   Their scent, and rustle down their perfumed showers
   Of bloom on the bent grass where I am laid,
   And bower me from the August sun with shade;
And the eye travels down to Oxford's towers.   30

And near me on the grass lies Glanvil's book—
   Come, let me read the oft-read tale again!
     The story of the Oxford scholar poor,
   Of pregnant parts and quick inventive brain,
     Who, tired of knocking at preferment's door,   35
      One summer-morn forsook

His friends, and went to learn the gipsy-lore,
  And roam'd the world with that wild brotherhood,
  And came, as most men deem'd, to little good,
But came to Oxford and his friends no more.   40

But once, years after, in the country-lanes,
  Two scholars, whom at college erst he knew,
  Met him, and of his way of life enquired;
Whereat he answer'd, that the gipsy-crew,
  His mates, had arts to rule as they desired   45
    The workings of men's brains,
And they can bind them to what thoughts they will.
  'And I,' he said, 'the secret of their art,
  When fully learn'd, will to the world impart;
But it needs heaven-sent moments for this skill.'   50

This said, he left them, and return'd no more.—
  But rumours hung about the country-side,
  That the lost Scholar long was seen to stray,
Seen by rare glimpses, pensive and tongue-tied,
  In hat of antique shape, and cloak of grey,   55
    The same the gipsies wore.
Shepherds had met him on the Hurst in spring;
  At some lone alehouse in the Berkshire moors,
  On the warm ingle-bench, the smock-frock'd boors
Had found him seated at their entering,   60

But, 'mid their drink and clatter, he would fly.
And I myself seem half to know thy looks,
  And put the shepherds, wanderer! on thy trace;
And boys who in lone wheatfields scare the rooks
  I ask if thou hast pass'd their quiet place;   65
    Or in my boat I lie

Moor'd to the cool bank in the summer-heats,
  'Mid wide grass meadows which the sunshine fills,
    And watch the warm, green-muffled Cumner hills,
  And wonder if thou haunt'st their shy retreats.   70

For most, I know, thou lov'st retired ground!
  Thee at the ferry Oxford riders blithe,
    Returning home on summer-nights, have met
  Crossing the stripling Thames at Bab-lock-hithe,
    Trailing in the cool stream thy fingers wet,   75
      As the punt's rope chops round;
  And leaning backward in a pensive dream,
    And fostering in thy lap a heap of flowers
    Pluck'd in shy fields and distant Wychwood bowers,
  And thine eyes resting on the moonlit stream.   80

And then they land, and thou art seen no more!—
  Maidens, who from the distant hamlets come
    To dance around the Fyfield elm in May,
  Oft through the darkening fields have seen thee roam,
    Or cross a stile into the public way.   85
      Oft thou hast given them store
  Of flowers—the frail-leaf'd, white anemony,
    Dark bluebells drench'd with dews of summer eves,
    And purple orchises with spotted leaves—
  But none hath words she can report of thee.   90

And, above Godstow Bridge, when hay-time's here
  In June, and many a scythe in sunshine flames,
    Men who through those wide fields of breezy grass
  Where black-wing'd swallows haunt the glittering Thames,
    To bathe in the abandon'd lasher pass,   95
      Have often pass'd thee near

Sitting upon the river bank o'ergrown;
　Mark'd thine outlandish garb, thy figure spare,
　Thy dark vague eyes, and soft abstracted air—
But, when they came from bathing, thou wast gone!　100

At some lone homestead in the Cumner hills,
　Where at her open door the housewife darns,
　　Thou hast been seen, or hanging on a gate
　To watch the threshers in the mossy barns.
　　Children, who early range these slopes and late　105
　　　For cresses from the rills,
　Have known thee eying, all an April-day,
　　The springing pastures and the feeding kine;
　　And mark'd thee, when the stars come out and shine
Through the long dewy grass move slow away.　110

In autumn, on the skirts of Bagley Wood—
　Where most the gipsies by the turf-edged way
　　Pitch their smoked tents, and every bush you see
　With scarlet patches tagg'd and shreds of grey,
　　Above the forest-ground called Thessaly—　115
　　　The blackbird, picking food,
　Sees thee, nor stops his meal, nor fears at all;
　　So often has he known thee past him stray,
　　Rapt, twirling in thy hand a wither'd spray,
And waiting for the spark from heaven to fall.　120

And once, in winter, on the causeway chill
　Where home through flooded fields foot-travellers go,
　　Have I not pass'd thee on the wooden bridge,
　Wrapt in thy cloak and battling with the snow,
　　Thy face tow'rd Hinksey and its wintry ridge?　125
　　　And thou hast climb'd the hill,

And gain'd the white brow of the Cumner range;
   Turn'd once to watch, while thick the snowflakes fall,
     The line of festal light in Christ-Church hall—
Then sought thy straw in some sequester'd grange.   130

But what—I dream! Two hundred years are flown
   Since first thy story ran through Oxford halls,
     And the grave Glanvil did the tale inscribe
That thou wert wander'd from the studious walls
     To learn strange arts, and join a gipsy-tribe;   135
       And thou from earth art gone
Long since, and in some quiet churchyard laid—
   Some country-nook, where o'er thy unknown grave
   Tall grasses and white flowering nettles wave,
Under a dark, red-fruited yew-tree's shade.   140

—No, no, thou hast not felt the lapse of hours!
   For what wears out the life of mortal men?
     'Tis that from change to change their being rolls;
   'Tis that repeated shocks, again, again,
     Exhaust the energy of strongest souls   145
       And numb the elastic powers.
Till having used our nerves with bliss and teen,
   And tired upon a thousand schemes our wit,
   To the just-pausing Genius we remit
Our worn-out life, and are—what we have been.   150

Thou hast not lived, why should'st thou perish, so?
   Thou hadst *one* aim, *one* business, *one* desire;
     Else wert thou long since number'd with the dead!
   Else hadst thou spent, like other men, thy fire!
     The generations of thy peers are fled,   155
       And we ourselves shall go;

But thou possessest an immortal lot,
 And we imagine thee exempt from age
 And living as thou liv'st on Glanvil's page,
Because thou hadst—what we, alas! have not. 160

For early didst thou leave the world, with powers
 Fresh, undiverted to the world without,
  Firm to their mark, not spent on other things;
 Free from the sick fatigue, the languid doubt, 164
  Which much to have tried, in much been baffled, brings.
   O life unlike to ours!
 Who fluctuate idly without term or scope,
  Of whom each strives, nor knows for what he strives,
  And each half lives a hundred different lives;
 Who wait like thee, but not, like thee, in hope. 170

Thou waitest for the spark from heaven! and we,
 Light half-believers of our casual creeds,
  Who never deeply felt, nor clearly will'd,
 Whose insight never has borne fruit in deeds,
  Whose vague resolves never have been fulfill'd; 175
   For whom each year we see
 Breeds new beginnings, disappointments new;
  Who hesitate and falter life away,
  And lose to-morrow the ground won to-day—
 Ah! do not we, wanderer! await it too? 180

Yes, we await it!—but it still delays,
 And then we suffer! and amongst us one,
  Who most has suffer'd, takes dejectedly
 His seat upon the intellectual throne;
  And all his store of sad experience he 185
   Lays bare of wretched days;

Tells us his misery's birth and growth and signs,
    And how the dying spark of hope was fed,
      And how the breast was soothed, and how the head,
    And all his hourly varied anodynes.   **190**

This for our wisest! and we others pine,
    And wish the long unhappy dream would end,
      And waive all claim to bliss, and try to bear;
    With close-lipp'd patience for our only friend,
      Sad patience, too near neighbour to despair—   **195**
        But none has hope like thine!
  Thou through the fields and through the woods dost stray,
    Roaming the country-side, a truant boy,
    Nursing thy project in unclouded joy,
  And every doubt long blown by time away.   **200**

O born in days when wits were fresh and clear,
    And life ran gaily as the sparkling Thames;
      Before this strange disease of modern life,
    With its sick hurry, its divided aims,
      Its heads o'ertax'd, its palsied hearts, was rife—   **205**
        Fly hence, our contact fear!
  Still fly, plunge deeper in the bowering wood!
    Averse, as Dido did with gesture stern
    From her false friend's approach in Hades turn,
  Wave us away, and keep thy solitude!   **210**

Still nursing the unconquerable hope,
    Still clutching the inviolable shade,
      With a free, onward impulse brushing through,
    By night, the silver'd branches of the glade—
      Far on the forest-skirts, where none pursue,   **215**
        On some mild pastoral slope

Emerge, and resting on the moonlit pales
   Freshen thy flowers as in former years
   With dew, or listen with enchanted ears,
From the dark dingles, to the nightingales!   220

But fly our paths, our feverish contact fly!
   For strong the infection of our mental strife,
      Which, though it gives no bliss, yet spoils for rest;
   And we should win thee from thy own fair life,
      Like us distracted, and like us unblest.   225
         Soon, soon thy cheer would die,
Thy hopes grow timorous, and unfix'd thy powers,
   And thy clear aims be cross and shifting made;
   And then thy glad perennial youth would fade,
Fade, and grow old at last, and die like ours.   230

Then fly our greetings, fly our speech and smiles!
   —As some grave Tyrian trader, from the sea,
      Descried at sunrise an emerging prow
Lifting the cool-hair'd creepers stealthily,
      The fringes of a southward-facing brow   235
         Among the Ægæan isles;
And saw the merry Grecian coaster come,
   Freighted with amber grapes and Chian wine,
   Green, bursting figs, and tunnies steep'd in brine—
And knew the intruders on his ancient home,

The young light-hearted masters of the waves—
   And snatch'd his rudder, and shook out more sail;
      And day and night held on indignantly
O'er the blue Midland waters with the gale,
      Betwixt the Syrtes and soft Sicily,   245
         To where the Atlantic raves

Outside the western straits; and unbent sails
  There, where down cloudy cliffs, through sheets of foam
  Shy traffickers, the dark Iberians come;
And on the beach undid his corded bales.   250

STANZAS FROM THE GRANDE CHARTREUSE

1855. *New Poems* (1867)

THROUGH Alpine meadows soft-suffused
With rain, where thick the crocus blows,
Past the dark forges long disused,
The mule-track from Saint Laurent goes.
The bridge is cross'd, and slow we ride,   5
Through forest, up the mountain-side.

The autumnal evening darkens round,
The wind is up, and drives the rain;
While, hark! far down, with strangled sound
Doth the Dead Guier's stream complain,   10
Where that wet smoke, among the woods,
Over his boiling cauldron broods.

Swift rush the spectral vapours white
Past limestone scars with ragged pines,
Showing—then blotting from our sight!—   15
Halt—through the cloud-drift something shines!
High in the valley, wet and drear,
The huts of Courrerie appear.

Strike leftward! cries our guide; and higher
Mounts up the stony forest-way.   20
At last the encircling trees retire;
Look! through the showery twilight grey
What pointed roofs are these advance?—
A palace of the Kings of France?

Approach, for what we seek is here!   25
Alight, and sparely sup, and wait
For rest in this outbuilding near;
Then cross the sward and reach that gate.
Knock; pass the wicket! Thou art come
To the Carthusians' world-famed home.   30

The silent courts, where night and day
Into their stone-carved basins cold
The splashing icy fountains play—
The humid corridors behold!
Where, ghostlike in the deepening night,   35
Cowl'd forms brush by in gleaming white.

The chapel, where no organ's peal
Invests the stern and naked prayer—
With penitential cries they kneel
And wrestle; rising then, with bare   40
And white uplifted faces stand,
Passing the Host from hand to hand;

Each takes, and then his visage wan
Is buried in his cowl once more.
The cells!—the suffering Son of Man   45
Upon the wall—the knee-worn floor—
And where they sleep, that wooden bed,
Which shall their coffin be, when dead!

The library, where tract and tome
Not to feed priestly pride are there,   50
To hymn the conquering march of Rome,
Nor yet to amuse, as ours are!
They paint of souls the inner strife,
Their drops of blood, their death in life.

The garden, overgrown—yet mild,　　　　55
See, fragrant herbs are flowering there!
Strong children of the Alpine wild
Whose culture is the brethren's care;
Of human tasks their only one,
And cheerful works beneath the sun.　　　60

Those halls, too, destined to contain
Each its own pilgrim-host of old,
From England, Germany, or Spain—
All are before me! I behold
The House, the Brotherhood austere!　　　65
—And what am I, that I am here?

For rigorous teachers seized my youth,
And purged its faith, and trimm'd its fire,
Show'd me the high, white star of Truth,
There bade me gaze, and there aspire.　　　70
Even now their whispers pierce the gloom:
What dost thou in this living tomb?

Forgive me, masters of the mind!
At whose behest I long ago
So much unlearnt, so much resign'd—　　　75
I come not here to be your foe!
I seek these anchorites, not in ruth,
To curse and to deny your truth;

Not as their friend, or child, I speak
But as, on some far northern strand,　　　80
Thinking of his own Gods, a Greek
In pity and mournful awe might stand
Before some fallen Runic stone—
For both were faiths, and both are gone.

Wandering between two worlds, one dead,   85
The other powerless to be born,
With nowhere yet to rest my head,
Like these, on earth I wait forlorn.
Their faith, my tears, the world deride—
I come to shed them at their side.   90

Oh, hide me in your gloom profound,
Ye solemn seats of holy pain!
Take me, cowl'd forms, and fence me round,
Till I possess my soul again;
Till free my thoughts before me roll,   95
Not chafed by hourly false control!

For the world cries your faith is now
But a dead time's exploded dream;
My melancholy, sciolists say,
Is a pass'd mode, an outworn theme—   100
As if the world had ever had
A faith, or sciolists been sad!

Ah, if it *be* pass'd, take away,
At least, the restlessness, the pain;
Be man henceforth no more a prey   105
To these out-dated stings again!
The nobleness of grief is gone—
Ah, leave us not the fret alone!

But—if you cannot give us ease—
Last of the race of them who grieve,   110
Here leave us to die out with these
Last of the people who believe!
Silent, while years engrave the brow;
Silent—the best are silent now.

Achilles ponders in his tent,   115
The kings of modern thought are dumb;
Silent they are, though not content,
And wait to see the future come.
They have the grief men had of yore,
But they contend and cry no more.   120

Our fathers water'd with their tears
This sea of time whereon we sail,
Their voices were in all men's ears
Who pass'd within their puissant hail.
Still the same ocean round us raves,   125
But we stand mute, and watch the waves.

For what avail'd it, all the noise
And outcry of the former men?—
Say, have their sons achieved more joys,
Say, is life lighter now than then?   130
The sufferers died, they left their pain—
The pangs which tortured them remain.

What helps it now, that Byron bore,
With haughty scorn which mock'd the smart,
Through Europe to the Ætolian shore   135
The pageant of his bleeding heart?
That thousands counted every groan,
—And Europe made his woe her own?

What boots it, Shelley! that the breeze
Carried thy lovely wail away,   140
Musical through Italian trees
Which fringe thy soft blue Spezzian bay?
Inheritors of thy distress
Have restless hearts one throb the less?

Or are we easier, to have read,   145
O Obermann! the sad, stern page,
Which tells us how thou hidd'st thy head
From the fierce tempest of thine age
In the lone brakes of Fontainebleau,
Or chalets near the Alpine snow?   150

Ye slumber in your silent grave!—
The world, which for an idle day
Grace to your mood of sadness gave,
Long since hath flung her weeds away.
The eternal trifler breaks your spell;   155
But we—we learnt your lore too well!

irreverent

Years hence, perhaps, may dawn an age,
More fortunate, alas! than we,
Which without hardness will be sage,
And gay without frivolity.   160
Sons of the world, oh, speed those years;
But, while we wait, allow our tears!

Allow them! We admire with awe
The exulting thunder of your race;
You give the universe your law,   165
You triumph over time and space!
Your pride of life, your tireless powers,
We laud them, but they are not ours.

We are like children rear'd in shade
Beneath some old-world abbey wall,   170
Forgotten in a forest-glade,
And secret from the eyes of all.
Deep, deep the greenwood round them waves,
Their abbey, and its close of graves!

But, where the road runs near the stream,   175
Oft through the trees they catch a glance
Of passing troops in the sun's beam—
Pennon, and plume, and flashing lance!
Forth to the world those soldiers fare,
To life, to cities, and to war!   180

And through the wood, another way,
Faint bugle-notes from far are borne,
Where hunters gather, staghounds bay,
Round some fair forest-lodge at morn.
Gay dames are there, in sylvan green;   185
Laughter and cries—those notes between!

The banners flashing through the trees
Make their blood dance and chain their eyes;
That bugle-music on the breeze
Arrests them with a charm'd surprise.   190
Banner by turns and bugle woo:
Ye shy recluses, follow too!

O children, what do ye reply?—
'Action and pleasure, will ye roam
Through these secluded dells to cry   195
And call us?—but too late ye come!
Too late for us your call ye blow,
Whose bent was taken long ago.

'Long since we pace this shadow'd nave;
We watch those yellow tapers shine,   200
Emblems of hope over the grave,
In the high altar's depth divine;
The organ carries to our ear
Its accents of another sphere.

95

'Fenced early in this cloistral round
Of reverie, of shade, of prayer,
How should we grow in other ground?
How can we flower in foreign air?
—Pass, banners, pass, and bugles, cease;
And leave our desert to its peace!'

210

RUGBY CHAPEL

1857? *New Poems* (1867)

COLDLY, sadly descends
The autumn-evening. The field
Strewn with its dank yellow drifts
Of wither'd leaves, and the elms,
Fade into dimness apace,   5
Silent;—hardly a shout
From a few boys late at their play!
The lights come out in the street,
In the school-room windows;—but cold,
Solemn, unlighted, austere,   10
Through the gathering darkness, arise
The chapel-walls, in whose bound
Thou, my father! art laid.

There thou dost lie, in the gloom
Of the autumn evening. But ah!   15
That word, *gloom*, to my mind
Brings thee back, in the light
Of thy radiant vigour, again;
In the gloom of November we pass'd
Days not dark at thy side;   20
Seasons impair'd not the ray
Of thy buoyant cheerfulness clear.
Such thou wast! and I stand
In the autumn evening, and think
Of bygone autumns with thee.   25

Fifteen years have gone round
Since thou arosest to tread,
In the summer-morning, the road
Of death, at a call unforeseen,
Sudden. For fifteen years,   30
We who till then in thy shade
Rested as under the boughs
Of a mighty oak, have endured
Sunshine and rain as we might,
Bare, unshaded, alone,   35
Lacking the shelter of thee.

O strong soul, by what shore
Tarriest thou now? For that force,
Surely, has not been left vain!
Somewhere, surely, afar,   40
In the sounding labour-house vast
Of being, is practised that strength,
Zealous, beneficent, firm!

Yes, in some far-shining sphere,
Conscious or not of the past,   45
Still thou performest the word
Of the Spirit in whom thou dost live—
Prompt, unwearied, as here!
Still thou upraisest with zeal
The humble good from the ground,   50
Sternly repressest the bad!
Still, like a trumpet, dost rouse
Those who with half-open eyes
Tread the border-land dim
'Twixt vice and virtue; reviv'st,   55
Succourest!—this was thy work,
This was thy life upon earth.

What is the course of the life
Of mortal men on the earth?—
Most men eddy about   60
Here and there—eat and drink,
Chatter and love and hate,
Gather and squander, are raised
Aloft, are hurl'd in the dust,
Striving blindly, achieving   65
Nothing; and then they die—
Perish;—and no one asks
Who or what they have been,
More than he asks what waves,
In the moonlit solitudes mild   70
Of the midmost Ocean, have swell'd,
Foam'd for a moment, and gone.

And there are some, whom a thirst
Ardent, unquenchable, fires,
Not with the crowd to be spent,   75
Not without aim to go round
In an eddy of purposeless dust,
Effort unmeaning and vain.
Ah yes! some of us strive
Not without action to die   80
Fruitless, but something to snatch
From dull oblivion, nor all
Glut the devouring grave!
We, we have chosen our path
Path to a clear-purposed goal,   85
Path of advance!—but it leads
A long, steep journey, through sunk
Gorges, o'er mountains in snow.
Cheerful, with friends, we set forth—
Then, on the height, comes the storm.   90
Thunder crashes from rock

To rock, the cataracts reply,
Lightnings dazzle our eyes.
Roaring torrents have breach'd
The track, the stream-bed descends   95
In the place where the wayfarer once
Planted his footstep—the spray
Boils o'er its borders! aloft
The unseen snow-beds dislodge
Their hanging ruin; alas,   100
Havoc is made in our train!
Friends, who set forth at our side,
Falter, are lost in the storm.
We, we only are left!
With frowning foreheads, with lips   105
Sternly compress'd, we strain on,
On—and at nightfall at last
Come to the end of our way,
To the lonely inn 'mid the rocks;
Where the gaunt and taciturn host   110
Stands on the threshold, the wind
Shaking his thin white hairs—
Holds his lantern to scan
Our storm-beat figures, and asks:
Whom in our party we bring?   115
Whom we have left in the snow?

Sadly we answer: We bring
Only ourselves! we lost
Sight of the rest in the storm.
Hardly ourselves we fought through,   120
Stripp'd, without friends, as we are.
Friends, companions, and train,
The avalanche swept from our side.

But thou would'st not *alone*
Be saved, my father! *alone*   125

Conquer and come to thy goal,
Leaving the rest in the wild.
We were weary, and we
Fearful, and we in our march
Fain to drop down and to die.   130
Still thou turnedst, and still
Beckonedst the trembler, and still
Gavest the weary thy hand.

If, in the paths of the world,
Stones might have wounded thy feet,   135
Toil or dejection have tried
Thy spirit, of that we saw
Nothing—to us thou wast still
Cheerful, and helpful, and firm!
Therefore to thee it was given   140
Many to save with thyself;
And, at the end of thy day,
O faithful shepherd! to come,
Bringing thy sheep in thy hand.

And through thee I believe   145
In the noble and great who are gone;
Pure souls honour'd and blest
By former ages, who else—
Such, so soulless, so poor,
Is the race of men whom I see—   150
Seem'd but a dream of the heart,
Seem'd but a cry of desire.
Yes! I believe that there lived
Others like thee in the past,
Not like the men of the crowd   155
Who all round me to-day
Bluster or cringe, and make life
Hideous, and arid, and vile;

But souls temper'd with fire,
Fervent, heroic, and good,   160
Helpers and friends of mankind.

Servants of God!—or sons
Shall I not call you? because
Not as servants ye knew
Your Father's innermost mind,   165
His, who unwillingly sees
One of his little ones lost—
Yours is the praise, if mankind
Hath not as yet in its march
Fainted, and fallen, and died!   170

See! In the rocks of the world
Marches the host of mankind,
A feeble, wavering line.
Where are they tending?—A God
Marshall'd them, gave them their goal.   175
Ah, but the way is so long!
Years they have been in the wild!
Sore thirst plagues them, the rocks,
Rising all round, overawe;
Factions divide them, their host   180
Threatens to break, to dissolve.
—Ah, keep, keep them combined!
Else, of the myriads who fill
That army, not one shall arrive;
Sole they shall stray; in the rocks   185
Stagger for ever in vain,
Die one by one in the waste.

Then, in such hour of need
Of your fainting, dispirited race,

Ye, like angels, appear,   190
Radiant with ardour divine!
Beacons of hope, ye appear!
Languor is not in your heart,
Weakness is not in your word,
Weariness not on your brow.   195
Ye alight in our van! at your voice,
Panic, despair, flee away.
Ye move through the ranks, recall
The stragglers, refresh the outworn,
Praise, re-inspire the brave!   200
Order, courage, return.
Eyes rekindling, and prayers,
Follow your steps as ye go.
Ye fill up the gaps in our files,
Strengthen the wavering line,   205
Stablish, continue our march,
On, to the bound of the waste,
On, to the City of God.

THYRSIS

1866. *New Poems* (1867)

How changed is here each spot man makes or fills!
  In the two Hinkseys nothing keeps the same;
    The village street its haunted mansion lacks
  And from the sign is gone Sibylla's name,
    And from the roofs the twisted chimney-stacks—   5
      Are ye too changed, ye hills?
  See, 'tis no foot of unfamiliar men
    To-night from Oxford up your pathway strays!
    Here came I often, often, in old days—
Thyrsis and I; we still had Thyrsis then.   10

Runs it not here, the track by Childsworth Farm,
 Past the high wood, to where the elm-tree crowns
  The hill behind whose ridge the sunset flames?
 The signal-elm, that looks on Ilsley Downs,   14
  The Vale, the three lone weirs, the youthful Thames?—
   This winter-eve is warm,
 Humid the air! leafless, yet soft as spring,
  The tender purple spray on copse and briers!
  And that sweet city with her dreaming spires,
 She needs not June for beauty's heightening,   20

Lovely all times she lies, lovely to-night!—
 Only, methinks, some loss of habit's power
  Befalls me wandering through this upland dim.
 Once pass'd I blindfold here, at any hour;
  Now seldom come I, since I came with him.   25
   That single elm-tree bright
 Against the west—I miss it! is it gone?
  We prized it dearly; while it stood, we said,
  Our friend, the Gipsy-Scholar, was not dead;
 While the tree lived, he in these fields lived on.   30

Too rare, too rare, grow now my visits here,
 But once I knew each field, each flower, each stick;
  And with the country-folk acquaintance made
 By barn in threshing-time, by new-built rick.
  Here, too, our shepherd-pipes we first assay'd.   35
   Ah me! this many a year
 My pipe is lost, my shepherd's holiday!
  Needs must I lose them, needs with heavy heart
  Into the world and wave of men depart; ·
 But Thyrsis of his own will went away.   40

It irk'd him to be here, he could not rest.
 He loved each simple joy the country yields,

He loved his mates; but yet he could not keep,
For that a shadow lour'd on the fields,
   Here with the shepherds and the silly sheep.   **45**
      Some life of men unblest
He knew, which made him droop, and fill'd his head.
   He went; his piping took a troubled sound
   Of storms that rage outside our happy ground;
He could not wait their passing, he is dead.   **50**

So, some tempestuous morn in early June,
   When the year's primal burst of bloom is o'er,
   Before the roses and the longest day—
   When garden-walks and all the grassy floor
     With blossoms red and white of fallen May   **55**
      And chestnut-flowers are strewn—
So have I heard the cuckoo's parting cry,
   From the wet field, through the vext garden-trees,
   Come with the volleying rain and tossing breeze:
   The bloom is gone, and with the bloom go I!   60

Too quick despairer, wherefore wilt thou go?
   Soon will the high Midsummer pomps come on,
   Soon will the musk carnations break and swell,
   Soon shall we have gold-dusted snapdragon,
     Sweet-William with his homely cottage-smell,   65
      And stocks in fragrant blow;
Roses that down the alleys shine afar,
   And open, jasmine-muffled lattices,
   And groups under the dreaming garden-trees,
And the full moon, and the white evening-star.   70

He hearkens not! light comer, he is flown!
   What matters it? next year he will return,
   And we shall have him in the sweet spring-days,

With whitening hedges, and uncrumpling fern,
   And blue-bells trembling by the forest-ways,   75
     And scent of hay new-mown.
But Thyrsis never more we swains shall see;
   See him come back, and cut a smoother reed,
   And blow a strain the world at last shall heed—
For Time, not Corydon, hath conquer'd thee!   80

Alack, for Corydon no rival now!—
   But when Sicilian shepherds lost a mate,
     Some good survivor with his flute would go,
   Piping a ditty sad for Bion's fate;
     And cross the unpermitted ferry's flow,   85
       And relax Pluto's brow,
And make leap up with joy the beauteous head
   Of Proserpine, among whose crowned hair
   Are flowers first open'd on Sicilian air,
And flute his friend, like Orpheus, from the dead.   90

O easy access to the hearer's grace
   When Dorian shepherds sang to Proserpine!
     For she herself had trod Sicilian fields,
   She knew the Dorian water's gush divine,
     She knew each lily white which Enna yields,   95
       Each rose with blushing face;
She loved the Dorian pipe, the Dorian strain.
   But ah, of our poor Thames she never heard!
   Her foot the Cumner cowslips never stirr'd;
And we should tease her with our plaint in vain!   100

Well! wind-dispersed and vain the words will be,
   Yet, Thyrsis, let me give my grief its hour
     In the old haunt, and find our tree-topp'd hill!
   Who, if not I, for questing here hath power?

I know the wood which hides the daffodil,   105
  I know the Fyfield tree,
I know what white, what purple fritillaries
  The grassy harvest of the river-fields,
  Above by Ensham, down by Sandford, yields,
And what sedged brooks are Thames's tributaries;   110

I know these slopes; who knows them if not I?—
  But many a dingle on the loved hill-side,
    With thorns once studded, old, white-blossom'd trees,
  Where thick the cowslips grew, and far descried
    High tower'd the spikes of purple orchises,   115
      Hath since our day put by
  The coronals of that forgotten time;
    Down each green bank hath gone the ploughboy's team,
    And only in the hidden brookside gleam
  Primroses, orphans of the flowery prime.   120

Where is the girl, who by the boatman's door,
  Above the locks, above the boating throng,
    Unmoor'd our skiff when through the Wytham flats,
  Red loosestrife and blond meadow-sweet among
    And darting swallows and light water-gnats,   125
      We track'd the shy Thames shore?
  Where are the mowers, who, as the tiny swell
    Of our boat passing heaved the river-grass,
    Stood with suspended scythe to see us pass?
  They all are gone, and thou art gone as well!   130

Yes, thou art gone! and round me too the night
  In ever-nearing circle weaves her shade.
    I see her veil draw soft across the day,
  I feel her slowly chilling breath invade   134
    The cheek grown thin, the brown hair sprent with grey;

I feel her finger light
Laid pausefully upon life's headlong train;—
   The foot less prompt to meet the morning dew,
   The heart less bounding at emotion new,
And hope, once crush'd, less quick to spring again.   140

And long the way appears, which seem'd so short
   To the less practised eye of sanguine youth;
    And high the mountain-tops, in cloudy air,
   The mountain-tops where is the throne of Truth,
    Tops in life's morning-sun so bright and bare!   145
     Unbreachable the fort
   Of the long-batter'd world uplifts its wall;
    And strange and vain the earthly turmoil grows,
    And near and real the charm of thy repose,
And night as welcome as a friend would fall.   150

But hush! the upland hath a sudden loss
   Of quiet!—Look, adown the dusk hill-side,
    A troop of Oxford hunters going home,
   As in old days, jovial and talking, ride!   154
    From hunting with the Berkshire hounds they come.
     Quick! let me fly, and cross
   Into yon farther field!—'Tis done; and see,
    Back'd by the sunset, which doth glorify
    The orange and pale violet evening-sky,
Bare on its lonely ridge, the Tree! the Tree!   160

I take the omen! Eve lets down her veil,
   The white fog creeps from bush to bush about,
    The west unflushes, the high stars grow bright,
   And in the scatter'd farms the lights come out.
    I cannot reach the signal-tree to-night,   165
     Yet, happy omen, hail!

Hear it from thy broad lucent Arno-vale
    (For there thine earth-forgetting eyelids keep
    The morningless and unawakening sleep
Under the flowery oleanders pale),   170

Hear it, O Thyrsis, still our tree is there!—
  Ah, vain! These English fields, this upland dim,
    These brambles pale with mist engarlanded,
  That lone, sky-pointing tree, are not for him;
    To a boon southern country he is fled,   175
      And now in happier air,
  Wandering with the great Mother's train divine
    (And purer or more subtle soul than thee,
    I trow, the mighty Mother doth not see)
  Within a folding of the Apennine,   180

Thou hearest the immortal chants of old!—
  Putting his sickle to the perilous grain
    In the hot cornfield of the Phrygian king,
  For thee the Litverses-song again
    Young Daphnis with his silver voice doth sing; 185
      Sings his Sicilian fold,
  His sheep, his hapless love, his blinded eyes—
    And how a call celestial round him rang,
    And heavenward from the fountain-brink he sprang,
  And all the marvel of the golden skies.   190

There thou art gone, and me thou leavest here
  Sole in these fields! yet will I not despair.
    Despair I will not, while I yet descry
  Neath the mild canopy of English air
    That lonely tree against the western sky.   195
      Still, still these slopes, 'tis clear,
  Our Gipsy-Scholar haunts, outliving thee!

Fields where soft sheep from cages pull the hay,
Woods with anemonies in flower till May,
Know him a wanderer still; then why not me?   200

A fugitive and gracious light he seeks,
    Shy to illumine; and I seek it too.
        This does not come with houses or with gold,
    With place, with honour, and a flattering crew;
        'Tis not in the world's market bought and sold—   205
            But the smooth-slipping weeks
    Drop by, and leave its seeker still untired;
        Out of the heed of mortals he is gone,
        He wends unfollow'd, he must house alone;
    Yet on he fares, by his own heart inspired.   210

Thou too, O Thyrsis, on like quest wast bound;
    Thou wanderedst with me for a little hour!
        Men gave thee nothing; but this happy quest,
    If men esteem'd thee feeble, gave thee power,
        If men procured thee trouble, gave thee rest.   215
            And this rude Cumner ground,
    Its fir-topped Hurst, its farms, its quiet fields,
        Here cam'st thou in thy jocund youthful time,
        Here was thine height of strength, thy golden prime!
    And still the haunt beloved a virtue yields.   220

What though the music of thy rustic flute
    Kept not for long its happy, country tone;
        Lost it too soon, and learnt a stormy note
    Of men contention-tost, of men who groan,   224
        Which task'd thy pipe too sore, and tired thy throat—
            It fail'd, and thou wast mute!
    Yet hadst thou alway visions of our light,
        And long with men of care thou couldst not stay,

And soon thy foot resumed its wandering way,
Left human haunt, and on alone till night.   230

Too rare, too rare, grow now my visits here!
　'Mid city-noise, not, as with thee of yore,
　　Thyrsis! in reach of sheep-bells is my home.
　—Then through the great town's harsh, heart-wearying
　　　roar,
　　Let in thy voice a whisper often come,   235
　　　To chase fatigue and fear:
　Why faintest thou? I wander'd till I died.
　Roam on! The light we sought is shining still.
　Dost thou ask proof? Our tree yet crowns the hill,
Our Scholar travels yet the loved hill-side.   240

AUSTERITY OF POETRY
New Poems (1867)

Tʜᴀᴛ son of Italy who tried to blow,
Ere Dante came, the trump of sacred song,
In his light youth amid a festal throng
Sate with his bride to see a public show.

Fair was the bride, and on her front did glow   5
Youth like a star; and what to youth belong—
Gay raiment, sparkling gauds, elation strong.
A prop gave way! crash fell a platform! lo,

'Mid struggling sufferers, hurt to death, she lay!
Shuddering, they drew her garments off—and found
A robe of sackcloth next the smooth, white skin. 11

Such, poets, is your bride, the Muse! young, gay,
Radiant, adorn'd outside; a hidden ground
Of thought and of austerity within.

DOVER BEACH

New Poems (1867)

THE sea is calm to-night.
The tide is full, the moon lies fair
Upon the straits;—on the French coast the light
Gleams and is gone; the cliffs of England stand,
Glimmering and vast, out in the tranquil bay.   5
Come to the window, sweet is the night-air!
Only, from the long line of spray
Where the sea meets the moon-blanch'd land,
Listen! you hear the grating roar
Of pebbles which the waves draw back, and fling,   10
At their return, up the high strand,
Begin, and cease, and then again begin,
With tremulous cadence slow, and bring
The eternal note of sadness in.

Sophocles long ago   15
Heard it on the Ægæan, and it brought
Into his mind the turbid ebb and flow
Of human misery; we
Find also in the sound a thought,
Hearing it by this distant northern sea.   20

The Sea of Faith
Was once, too, at the full, and round earth's shore
Lay like the folds of a bright girdle furl'd.
But now I only hear
Its melancholy, long, withdrawing roar,   25
Retreating, to the breath
Of the night-wind, down the vast edges drear
And naked shingles of the world.

Ah, love, let us be true
To one another! for the world, which seems   30
To lie before us like a land of dreams,
So various, so beautiful, so new,
Hath really neither joy, nor love, nor light,
Nor certitude, nor peace, nor help for pain;
And we are here as on a darkling plain   35
Swept with confused alarms of struggle and flight,
Where ignorant armies clash by night.

BACCHANALIA;

OR,

THE NEW AGE

New Poems (1867)

I

THE evening comes, the fields are still.
The tinkle of the thirsty rill,
Unheard all day, ascends again;
Deserted is the half-mown plain,
Silent the swaths! the ringing wain,   5
The mower's cry, the dog's alarms,
All housed within the sleeping farms!
The business of the day is done,
The last-left haymaker is gone.
And from the thyme upon the height,   10
And from the elder blossom white
And pale dog-roses in the hedge,
And from the mint-plant in the sedge,
In puffs of balm the night-air blows
The perfume which the day forgoes.   15
And on the pure horizon far,
See, pulsing with the first-born star,
The liquid sky above the hill!
The evening comes, the fields are still.

Loitering and leaping,   20
With saunter, with bounds —
Flickering and circling
In files and in rounds—
Gaily their pine-staff green
Tossing in air,   25
Loose o'er their shoulders white
Showering their hair—
See! the wild Mænads
Break from the wood,
Youth and Iacchus   30
Maddening their blood.
See! through the quiet land
Rioting they pass—
Fling the fresh heaps about,
Trample the grass.   35
Tear from the rifled hedge
Garlands, their prize;
Fill with their sports the field,
Fill with their cries.

Shepherd, what ails thee, then?   40
Shepherd, why mute?
Forth with thy joyous song!
Forth with thy flute!
Tempts not the revel blithe?
Lure not their cries?   45
Glow not their shoulders smooth?
Melt not their eyes?
Is not, on cheeks like those,
Lovely the flush?
—*Ah, so the quiet was!*   50
So was the hush!

II

The epoch ends, the world is still.
The age has talk'd and work'd its fill—
The famous orators have shone,
The famous poets sung and gone,   55
The famous men of war have fought,
The famous speculators thought,
The famous players, sculptors, wrought,
The famous painters fill'd their wall,
The famous critics judged it all.   60
The combatants are parted now—
Uphung the spear, unbent the bow,
The puissant crown'd, the weak laid low.
And in the after-silence sweet,
Now strifes are hush'd, our ears doth meet,   65
Ascending pure, the bell-like fame
Of this or that down-trodden name
Delicate spirits, push'd away
In the hot press of the noon-day.
And o'er the plain, where the dead age   70
Did its now silent warfare wage—
O'er that wide plain, now wrapt in gloom,
Where many a splendour finds its tomb,
Many spent fames and fallen mights—
The one or two immortal lights   75
Rise slowly up into the sky
To shine there everlastingly,
Like stars over the bounding hill.
The epoch ends, the world is still.

> Thundering and bursting   80
> In torrents, in waves—
> Carolling and shouting
> Over tombs, amid graves—

See! on the cumber'd plain
Clearing a stage,   85
Scattering the past about,
Comes the new age.
Bards make new poems,
Thinkers new schools,
Statesmen new systems,   90
Critics new rules.
All things begin again;
Life is their prize;
Earth with their deeds they fill,
Fill with their cries.   95

Poet, what ails thee, then?
Say, why so mute?
Forth with thy praising voice!
Forth with thy flute!
Loiterer! why sittest thou   100
Sunk in thy dream?
Tempts not the bright new age?
Shines not its stream?
Look, ah, what genius,
Art, science, wit!   105
Soldiers like Cæsar,
Statesmen like Pitt!
Sculptors like Phidias,
Raphaels in shoals,
Poets like Shakespeare—   110
Beautiful souls!
See, on their glowing cheeks
Heavenly the flush!
—*Ah, so the silence was!*
So was the hush!   115

The world but feels the present's spell,
The poet feels the past as well;
Whatever men have done, might do,
Whatever thought, might think it too.

A WISH

New Poems (1867)

I ASK not that my bed of death
From bands of greedy heirs be free;
For these besiege the latest breath
Of fortune's favour'd sons, not me.

I ask not each kind soul to keep   5
Tearless, when of my death he hears.
Let those who will, if any, weep!
There are worse plagues on earth than tears.

I ask but that my death may find
The freedom to my life denied;   10
Ask but the folly of mankind
Then, then at last, to quit my side.

Spare me the whispering, crowded room,
The friends who come, and gape, and go;
The ceremonious air of gloom—   15
All, which makes death a hideous show!

Nor bring, to see me cease to live,
Some doctor full of phrase and fame,
To shake his sapient head, and give
The ill he cannot cure a name.   20

Nor fetch, to take the accustom'd toll
Of the poor sinner bound for death,
His brother-doctor of the soul,
To canvass with official breath

The future and its viewless things—   **25**
That undiscover'd mystery
Which one who feels death's winnowing wings
Must needs read clearer, sure, than he!

Bring none of these; but let me be,
While all around in silence lies,   **30**
Moved to the window near, and see
Once more, before my dying eyes,

Bathed in the sacred dews of morn
The wide aerial landscape spread—
The world which was ere I was born,   **35**
The world which lasts when I am dead;

Which never was the friend of *one*,
Nor promised love it could not give,
But lit for all its generous sun,
And lived itself, and made us live.   **40**

There let me gaze, till I become
In soul, with what I gaze on, wed!
To feel the universe my home;
To have before my mind—instead

Of the sick room, the mortal strife,   **45**
The turmoil for a little breath—
The pure eternal course of life,
Not human combatings with death!

Thus feeling, gazing, might I grow
Composed, refresh'd, ennobled, clear;   50
Then willing let my spirit go
To work or wait elsewhere or here!

THE LAST WORD

New Poems (1867)

CREEP into thy narrow bed,
Creep, and let no more be said!
Vain thy onset! all stands fast.
Thou thyself must break at last.

Let the long contention cease!   5
Geese are swans, and swans are geese.
Let them have it how they will!
Thou art tired; best be still.

They out-talk'd thee, hiss'd thee, tore thee?
Better men fared thus before thee;   10
Fired their ringing shot and pass'd,
Hotly charged—and sank at last.

Charge once more, then, and be dumb!
Let the victors, when they come,
When the forts of folly fall,   15
Find thy body by the wall!

A SPEECH AT ETON

1879. *Irish Essays* (1882)

THE philosopher Epictetus, who had a school at Nicopolis in
Epirus at the end of the first century of our era, thus apostro-
phises a young gentleman whom he supposes to be applying
to him for education:—

'Young sir, at home you have been at fisticuffs with the
man-servant, you have turned the house upside down, you
have been a nuisance to the neighbours; and do you come
here with the composed face of a sage, and mean to sit in
judgment upon the lesson, and to criticise my want of point?
10 You have come in here with envy and chagrin in your heart,
humiliated at not getting your allowance paid you from
home; and you sit with your mind full, in the intervals of the
lecture, of how your father behaves to you, and how your
brother. What are the people down at home saying about
me?—They are thinking: Now he is getting on! they are
saying: He will come home a walking dictionary!—Yes, and
I should like to go home a walking dictionary; but then there
is a deal of work required, and nobody sends me anything,
and the bathing here at Nicopolis is dirty and nasty; things
20 are all bad at home, and all bad here.'

Nobody can say that the bathing at Eton is dirty and
nasty. But at Eton, as at Nicopolis, the moral disposition
in which the pupil arrives at school, the thoughts and habits
which he brings with him from home and from the social
order in which he moves, must necessarily affect his power
of profiting by what his schoolmasters have to teach him.
This necessity is common to all schooling. You cannot
escape from it here any more than they could at Nicopolis.

Epictetus, however, was fully persuaded that what he had
30 to teach was valuable, if the mental and moral frame of his

pupils were but healthy enough to permit them to profit by it. I hope the Eton masters have the same conviction as to the native value of what they teach. But you know how many doubters and deniers of the value of a classical education we nowadays meet with. Let us put aside all that is said of the idleness, extravagance, and self-indulgence of the schoolboy. This may pair off with the complaint of Epictetus about the unsatisfactory moral state of his pupil. But with us there are many people who go on and say: 'And when the schoolboy, in our public schools, does learn, he learns nothing that is worth knowing.'

It is not of the Eton schoolboy only that this is said, but of the public schoolboy generally. We are all in the same boat,—all of us in whose schooling the Greek and Latin classics fill the principal place. And it avails nothing, that you try and appease the gainsayer by now acquainting yourselves with the diameter of the sun and moon, and with all sorts of matters which to us of an earlier and ruder generation were unknown. So long as the Greek and Latin classics continue to fill, as they do fill, the chief place in your school-work, the gainsayer is implacable and sticks to his sentence: 'When the boy does learn, he learns nothing that is worth knowing.'

Amidst all this disparagement, one may well ask oneself anxiously what is really to be said on behalf of studies over which so much of our time is spent, and for which we have, many of us, contracted a fondness. And after much consideration I have arrived at certain conclusions, which for my own use I find sufficient, but which are of such extreme simplicity that one ought to hesitate, perhaps, before one produces them to other people. However, such as they are, I have been led to bring them out more than once, and I will very briefly rehearse them now. It seems to me, firstly, that what a man seeks through his education is to get to know himself and the world; next, that for this knowledge it is

before all things necessary that he acquaint himself with
the best which has been thought and said in the world;
finally, that of this *best* the classics of Greece and Rome
form a very chief portion, and the portion most entirely
satisfactory. With these conclusions lodged safe in one's
mind, one is staunch on the side of the humanities.

And in the same spirit of simplicity in which these conclusions have been reached, I proceed further. People complain that the significance of the classics which we read at
10 school is not enough brought out, that the whole order and
sense of that world from which they issue is not seized and
held up to view. Well, but the best, in literature, has the
quality of being in itself formative,—silently formative; of
bringing out its own significance as we read it. It is better
to read a masterpiece much, even if one does that only,
than to read it a little, and to be told a great deal about its
significance, and about the development and sense of the
world from which it issues. Sometimes what one is told
about the significance of a work, and about the development
20 of a world, is extremely questionable. At any rate, a schoolboy, who, as they did in the times of ignorance at Eton, read
his Homer and Horace through, and then read them through
again, and so went on until he knew them by heart, is not,
in my opinion, so very much to be pitied.

Still that sounding phrase, 'the order and sense of a
world,' sends a kind of thrill through us when we hear it,
especially when the world spoken of is a thing so great and
so interesting as the Græco-Roman world of antiquity. If
we are not deluded by it into thinking that to read fine talk
30 about our classical documents is as good as to read the
documents themselves, the phrase is one which we may with
advantage lay to heart. I remember being struck, long ago,
with a remark on the Greek poet Theognis by Goethe, who
did not know Greek well and had to pick out its meaning by
the help of a Latin translation, but who brought to every-

thing which he read his powerful habits of thought and
criticism. 'When I first read Theognis,' says Goethe, in
substance, 'I thought him querulous and morbid, and disliked him. But when I came to know how entirely his poetry
proceeded from the real circumstances of his life, from the
situation of parties in Megara, his native city, and from the
effects of that situation upon himself and his friends, then
I read him with quite another feeling.' How very little do
any of us treat the poetry of Theognis and other ancients
in that fashion! was my thought after reading Goethe's 10
criticism. And earlier still I remember being struck at hearing a schoolfellow, who had left the sixth form at Rugby for
Cambridge, and who had fallen in somewhere with one of
Bunsen's sons, who is now a member of the German Parliament,—at hearing this schoolfellow contrast the training of
George Bunsen, as we then called him, with our own. Perhaps you think that at Rugby, which is often spoken of,
though quite erroneously, as a sort of opposition establishment to Eton, we treated the classics in a high philosophical
way, and traced the sequence of things in ancient literature, 20
when you at Eton professed nothing of the kind. But hear
the criticism of my old schoolfellow. 'It is wonderful,' said
he; 'not only can George Bunsen construe his Herodotus,
but he has a view of the place of Herodotus in literary
history, a thing none of us ever thought about.' My friend
spoke the truth; but even then, as I listened to him, I felt
an emotion at hearing of the place of Herodotus in literary
history. Yes, not only to be able to read the admirable
works of classical literature, but to conceive also that
Græco-Roman world, which is so mighty a factor in our own 30
world, our own life, to conceive it as a whole of which we can
trace the sequence, and the sense, and the connexion with
ourselves, this does undoubtedly also belong to a classical
education, rightly understood.

But even here, too, a plain person can proceed, if he

likes, with great simplicity. As Goethe says of life: Strike
into it anywhere, lay hold of it anywhere, it is always powerful and interesting,—so one may almost say of classical
literature. Strike into it where you like, lay hold of it where
you like, you can nearly always find a thread which will
lead you, if you follow it, to large and instructive results.
Let us to-night follow a single Greek word in this fashion,
and try to compensate ourselves, however imperfectly, for
having to divert our thoughts, just for one evening's lecture,
10 from the diameter of the sun and moon.

The word I will take is the word *eutrapelos, eutrapelia.*
Let us consider it first as it occurs in the famous Funeral
Oration put by Thucydides into the mouth of Pericles. The
word stands there for one of the chief of those qualities
which have made Athens, says Pericles, 'the school of
Greece;' for a quality by which Athens is eminently representative of what is called Hellenism: the quality of flexibility. 'A happy and gracious flexibility,' Pericles calls this
quality of the Athenians; and it is no doubt a charming gift.
20 Lucidity of thought, clearness and propriety of language,
freedom from prejudice and freedom from stiffness, open-
ness of mind, amiability of manners, all these seem to go
along with a certain happy flexibility of nature, and to
depend upon it. Nor does this suppleness and flexibility
of nature at all necessarily imply, as we English are apt
to suppose, a relaxed moral fibre and weakness. In the
Athenian of the best time it did not. 'In the Athenians,'
says Professor Curtius, 'the sense of energy abhorred every
kind of waste of time, their sense of measure abhorred bom-
30 bast and redundancy, and their clear intelligence everything
partaking of obscurity or vagueness; it was their habit in
all things to advance directly and resolutely to the goal.
Their dialect is characterised by a superior seriousness,
manliness, and vigour of language.'

There is no sign of relaxation of moral fibre here; and
yet, at the same time, the Athenians were eminent for a
happy and gracious flexibility. That quality, as we all know,
is not a characteristic quality of the Germanic nations, to
which we ourselves belong. Men are educable, and when we
read of the abhorrence of the Attic mind for redundancy and
obscurity of expression, its love for direct and telling speech,
and then think of modern German, we may say with satisfaction that the circumstances of our life have at any rate
educated us into the use of straightforward and vigorous 10
forms of language. But they have not educated us into
flexibility. All around us we may observe proofs of it. The
state of Ireland is a proof of it. We are rivals with Russia in
Central Asia, and at this moment it is particularly interesting to note, how the want of just this one Athenian quality
of flexibility seems to tell against us in our Asiatic rivalry
with Russia. 'Russia,' observes one who is perhaps the first
of living geographers,—an Austrian, Herr von Hellwald,—
'possesses far more shrewdness, *flexibility*, and congeniality
than England; qualities adapted to make the Asiatic more 20
tractable.' And again: 'There can be no dispute which of
the two, England or Russia, is the more civilised nation.
But it is just as certain that the highly civilised English
understand but indifferently how to raise their Asiatic subjects to their own standard of civilisation; whilst the
Russians attain, with their much lower standard of civilisation, far greater results amongst the Asiatic tribes, whom
they know how to assimilate in the most remarkable manner.
Of course they can only bring them to the same level which
they have reached themselves; but the little which they can 30
and do communicate to them counts actually for much
more than the great boons which the English do not know
how to impart. Under the auspices of Russia the advance
in civilisation amongst the Asiatics is indeed slow and in-
considerable, but steady, and suitable to their natural

capacities and the disposition of their race. On the other hand, they remain indifferent to British civilization, which is absolutely incomprehensible to them.'

Our word 'flexibility' has here carried us a long way, carried us to Turkestan and the valleys of the Jaxartes and Oxus. Let us get back to Greece, at any rate. The generation of Pericles is succeeded by the generation of Plato and Aristotle. Still the charming and Athenian quality of *eutrapelia* continues to be held in high esteem. Only the 10 word comes to stand more particularly for flexibility and felicity in the give-and-take of gay and light social intercourse. With Aristotle it is one of the virtues: the virtue of him who in this pleasant sort of intercourse, so relished by the Greeks, manages exactly to hit the happy and right mean; the virtue opposed to buffoonery on the one side, and to morose rusticity, or clownishness, on the other. It is in especial the virtue of the young, and is akin to the grace and charm of youth. When old men try to adapt themselves to the young, says Plato, they betake themselves, in imita-20 tion of the young, to *eutrapelia* and pleasantry.

Four hundred years pass, and we come to the date of the Epistle to the Ephesians. The word *eutrapelia* rises in the mind of the writer of that Epistle. It rises to St. Paul's mind, and he utters it; but in how different a sense from the praising and admiring sense in which we have seen the word used by Thucydides and Aristotle! *Eutrapelia*, which once stood for that eminently Athenian and Hellenic virtue of happy and gracious flexibility, now conveys this favourable sense no longer, but is ranked, with filthiness and foolish 30 talking, among things which are not convenient. Like these, it is not to be even so much as once named among the followers of God: 'neither filthiness, nor foolish talking, nor jesting (*eutrapelia*), which are not convenient.'

This is an extraordinary change, you will say. But now, as we have descended four hundred years from Aristotle to

St. Paul, let us ascend, not four hundred, not quite even one hundred years, from Thucydides to Pindar. The religious Theban poet, we shall see (and the thing is surely very remarkable), speaks of the quality of *eutrapelia* in the same disapproving and austere way as the writer of the Epistle to the Ephesians. The young and noble Jason appears at Iolcos, and being questioned about himself by Pelias, he answers that he has been trained in the nurture and admonition of the old and just Centaur, Chiron. 'From his cave I come, from Chariclo and Philyra, his stainless daughters, who there nursed me. Lo, these twenty years am I with them, and there hath been found in me neither deed nor word that is not convenient; and now, behold, I am come home, that I may recover my father's kingdom.' The adjective *eutrapelos*, as it is here used in connexion with its two nouns, means exactly a word or deed, in Biblical phrase, *of vain lightness*, a word or deed *such as is not convenient*.

There you have the history of the varying use of the words *eutrapelos, eutrapelia*. And now see how this varying use gives us a clue to the order and sense, as we say, of all that Greek world, so nearly and wonderfully connected with us, so profoundly interesting for us, so full of precious lessons.

We must begin with generalities, but we will try not to lose ourselves in them, and not to remain amongst them long. Human life and human society arise, we know, out of the presence in man of certain needs, certain instincts, and out of the constant endeavour of these instincts to satisfy and develope themselves. We may briefly sum them up, these needs or instincts, as being, first and foremost, a general instinct of expansion; then, as being instincts following diverse great lines, which may be conveniently designated as the lines of conduct, of intellect and knowledge, of beauty, of social life and manners. Some lines are more in view and more in honour at one time, some at another. Some men and some nations are more eminent on one line, some on another. But the final aim, of making our own and of harmoniously combining the powers to be reached on each and all of these great lines, is the ideal of human life. And our race is for ever recalled to this aim, and held fast to it, by the instinct of self-preservation in humanity.

The ideal of human life being such as it is, all these great and diverse powers, to the attainment of which our instincts, 10 as we have seen, impel us, hang together,—cannot be truly possessed and employed in isolation. Yet it is convenient, owing to the way in which we find them actually exhibiting themselves in human life and in history, to treat them separately, and to make distinctions of rank amongst them. In this view, we may say that the power of conduct is the greatest of all the powers now named; that it is even three-fourths of life. And wherever much is founded amongst men, there the power of conduct has surely been present and at work, although of course there may be and are, along with 20 it, other powers too.

Now, then, let us look at the beginnings of that Greece to which we owe so much, and which we may almost, so far as our intellectual life is concerned, call the mother of us all. 'So well has she done her part,' as the Athenian Isocrates truly says of her, 'that the name of Greeks seems no longer to stand for a race, but to stand for intelligence itself; and they who share in Hellenic culture are called Greeks even before those who are merely of Hellenic blood.' The beginnings of this wonderful Greece, what are they?

30 Greek history begins for us with the sanctuaries of Tempe and Delphi, and with the Apolline worship and priesthood which in those sanctuaries under Olympus and Parnassus established themselves. The northern sanctuary of Tempe soon yielded to Delphi as the centre of national Hellenic life and of Apolline religion. We are accustomed to think of

Apollo as the awakener and nourisher of what is called genius, and so from the very first the Greeks, too, considered him. But in those earliest days of Hellas, and at Delphi, where the hardy and serious tribes of the Dorian highlands made their influence felt, Apollo was not only the nourisher of genius, he was also the author of every higher moral effort. He was the prophet of his father Zeus, in the highest view of Zeus, as the source of the ideas of moral order and of right. For to this higher significance had the names of Zeus and Phœbus, names originally derived from sun and air,— gradually risen. They had come to designate a Father, the source of the ideas of moral order and of right; and a Son, his prophet, purifying and inspiring the soul with these ideas, and also with the idea of intellectual beauty.

Now, the ideas of moral order and of right which are in human nature, and which are, indeed, a main part of human life, were especially, we are told, a treasure possessed by the less gay and more solitary tribes in the mountains of Northern Greece. These Dorian tribes were Delphi's first pupils. And the graver view of life, the thoughts which give depth and solemnity to man's consciousness, the moral ideas, in short, of conduct and righteousness, were the governing elements in the manner of spirit propagated from Delphi. The words written up on the temple at Delphi called all comers to *soberness and righteousness*. The Doric and Æolic Pindar felt profoundly this severe influence of Delphi. It is not to be considered as an influence at war with the idea of intellectual beauty;—to mention the name of Pindar is in itself sufficient to show how little this was, or could be, the case. But it was, above all, an influence charged with the ideas of moral order and of right.

And there were confronting these Dorian founders of Hellas, and well known to them, and connected with them in manifold ways, other Greeks of a very different spiritual type; the Asiatic Greeks of Ionia, full of brilliancy and

mobility, but over whom the ideas of moral order and of
right had too little power, and who could never succeed in
founding among themselves a serious and powerful state. It
was evident that the great source of the incapacity which
accompanied, in these Ionians of Asia, so much brilliancy,
that the great enemy in them to the *Halt*, as Goethe calls it,
the steadiness, which moral natures so highly prize, was their
extreme mobility of spirit, their gay lightness, their *eutrapelia*. For Pindar, therefore, the word *eutrapelos*, expressing
10 easy flexibility and mobility, becomes a word of stern oppro-
brium, and conveys the reproach of vain folly.

The Athenians were Ionians. But they were Ionians
transplanted to Hellas, and who had breathed, as a Hellenic
nation, the air of Delphi, that bracing atmosphere of the
ideas of moral order and of right. In this atmosphere the
Athenians, Ionian as they were, imbibed influences of
character and steadiness, which for a long while balanced
their native vivacity and mobility, distinguished them profoundly from the Ionians of Asia, and gave them men like
20 Aristides.

Still, the Athenians were Ionians. They had the Ionian
quickness and flexibility, the Ionian turn for gaiety, wit, and
fearless thinking, the Ionian impatience of restraint. This
nature of theirs asserted itself, first of all, as an impatience
of *false* restraint. It asserted itself in opposition to the real
faults of the Dorian spirit,—faults which became more and
more manifest as time went on to the unprogressiveness of
this spirit, to its stiffness, hardness, narrowness, prejudice,
want of insight, want of amiability. And in real truth, by
30 the time of Pericles, Delphi, the great creation of the Dorian
spirit, had broken down, and was a witness to that spirit's
lack of a real power of life and growth. Bribes had dis-
credited the sanctity of Delphi; seriousness and vital power
had left it. It had come to be little more than a name, and
what continued to exist there was merely a number of forms.

Now then was the turn of the Athenians. With the idea of conduct, so little grasped by the Ionians of Asia, still deeply impressed on their soul, they freely and joyfully called forth also that pleasure in life, that love of clear thinking and of fearless discussion, that gay social temper, that ease and lightness, that gracious flexibility, which were in their nature. These were their gifts, and they did well to bring them forth. The gifts are in themselves gifts of great price, like those other gifts contributed by the primitive and serious Dorian tribes, their rivals. Man has to advance, we 10 have seen, along several lines, and he does well to advance along them. 'In the morning sow thy seed, and in the evening withhold not thine hand; for thou knowest not whether shall prosper, either this or that, or whether they both shall be alike good.'

And at this moment Thucydides, a man in whom the old virtue and the new reason were in just balance, has put into the mouth of Pericles, another man of the same kind, an encomium on the modern spirit, as we may call it, of which Athens was the representative. By the mouth of 20 Pericles, Thucydides condemned old-fashioned narrowness and illiberality. He applauded enjoyment of life. He applauded freedom from restraint. He applauded clear and fearless thinking,—the resolute bringing of our actions to the rule of reason. His expressions on this point greatly remind me of the fine saying of one of your own worthies, 'the ever-memorable Mr. John Hales, of Eton College.' 'I comprise it all,' says Hales, 'in two words: *what* and *wherefore*. That part of your burden which contains *what*, you willingly take up. But that other, which comprehends *why*, 30 that is either too hot or too heavy; you dare not meddle with it. But I must add that also to your burden, or else I must leave you for idle persons; for without the knowledge of *why*, of the grounds or reasons of things, there is no possibility of not being deceived.' It seems to me not improbable that Hales had here in his mind the very words of the Funeral Oration: 'We do not esteem discussion a hurt to action; what we consider mischievous is rather the setting oneself to work without first getting the guidance of reason.' Finally, Thucydides applauded the quality of nature which above all others made the Athenians the men for the new era, and he used the word *eutrapelos* in its proper and natural sense, to denote the quality of happy and gracious flexibility.

Somewhat narrowed, so as to mean especially flexibility 10 and adroitness in light social intercourse, but still employed in its natural and favourable sense, the word descends, as we saw, to Plato and Aristotle. Isocrates speaks of the quality as one which the old school regarded with alarm and disapproval; but, nevertheless, for him too the word has evidently, in itself, just the same natural and favourable sense which it has for Aristotle and Plato.

I quoted, just now, some words from the Book of Ecclesiastes, one of the wisest and one of the worst understood books in the Bible. Let us hear how the writer goes on after 20 the words which I quoted. He proceeds thus: 'Truly the light is sweet, and a pleasant thing it is for the eyes to behold the sun; yea, if a man live many years, let him rejoice in them all; and let him remember the days of darkness, for they shall be many. All that is future is vanity. Rejoice, O young man, in thy youth, and let thy heart cheer thee in the days of thy youth, and walk in the ways of thine heart and in the sight of thine eyes;—but know thou that for all these things God will bring thee into judgment.' Let us apply these admirable words to the life and work of the 30 Athenian people.

The old rigid order, in Greece, breaks down; a new power appears on the scene. It is the Athenian genius, with its freedom from restraint, its flexibility, its bold reason, its keen enjoyment of life. Well, let it try what it can do. Up to a certain point it is clearly in the right; possibly it may be in

the right altogether. Let it have free play, and show what
it can do. 'In the morning sow thy seed, and in the evening
withhold not thine hand; for thou knowest not whether shall
prosper, either this or that, or whether they both shall be
alike good.' Whether the old line is good, or the new line, or
whether they are both of them good, and must both of them
be used, cannot be known without trying. Let the Athenians
try, therefore, and let their genius have full swing. 'Rejoice;
walk in the ways of thine heart and in the sight of thine eyes;
—*but know thou that for all these things God will bring thee into* 10
judgment.' In other words: Your enjoyment of life, your freedom from restraint, your clear and bold reason, your flexibility, are natural and excellent; but on condition that you
know how to live with them, that you make a real success
of them.

And a man like Pericles or Phidias seemed to afford promise that Athens would know how to make a real success of
her qualities, and that an alliance between the old morality
and the new freedom might be, through the admirable Athenian genius, happily established. And with such promise 20
before his eyes, a serious man like Thucydides might well
give, to the new freedom, the high and warm praise which
we see given to it in the Funeral Oration.

But it soon became evident that the balance between the
old morality and the new freedom was not to be maintained,
and that the Athenians had the defects, as the saying is, of
their qualities. Their minds were full of other things than
those ideas of moral order and of right on which primitive
Hellas had formed itself, and of which they themselves had,
as worshippers in the shadow of the Parnassian sanctuary, 30
once deeply felt the power. These ideas lost their predominance. The predominance for Athens,—and, indeed, for
Hellas at large,—of a national religion of righteousness, of
grave ideas of conduct and moral order, predominating over
all other ideas, disappeared with the decline of Delphi, never

to return. Not only did these ideas lose exclusive predominance, they lost all due weight. Still, indeed, they inspired
poetry; and then, after inspiring the great Attic poets,
Æschylus and Sophocles, they inspired the great Attic philo-
sophers, Socrates and Plato. But the Attic nation, which
henceforth stood, in fact, for the Hellenic people, could not
manage to keep its mind bent sufficiently upon them. The
Attic nation had its mind bent on other things. It threw
itself ardently upon other lines, which man, indeed, has to
10 follow, which at one time, in Greece, had not been enough
followed, of which Athens strongly felt the attraction, and
on which it had rare gifts for excelling. The Attic nation
gave its heart to those powers which we have designated,
for the sake of brevity and convenience, as those of expansion, intellect, beauty, social life and manners. Athens and
Greece allowed themselves to be diverted and distracted
from attention to conduct, and to the ideas which inspire
conduct.

It was not that the old religious beliefs of Greece, to which
20 the ideas that inspire conduct had attached themselves, did
not require to be transformed by the new spirit. They did.
The greatest and best Hellenic souls, Anaxagoras, Pericles,
Phidias, Sophocles, Socrates, Plato, felt, and rightly felt,
that they did. The judicious historian of Greece, whom I
have already quoted, Professor Curtius, says expressly: 'The
popular faith was everywhere shaken, and a life resting
simply on the traditionary notions was no longer possible.
A dangerous rupture was at hand, unless the ancient faith
were purged and elevated in such a manner as to meet the
30 wants of the age. Mediators in this sense appeared in the
persons of the great poets of Athens.' Yes, they appeared;
but the current was setting too strongly another way. Poetry
itself, after the death of Sophocles, 'was seized,' says Professor Curtius, 'by the same current which dissolved the
foundations of the people's life, and which swept away the

soil wherein the emotions of the classical period had been rooted. The old perished; but the modern age, with all its readiness in thought and speech, was incapable of creating a new art as a support to its children.'

Socrates was so penetrated with the new intellectual spirit that he was called a sophist. But the great effort of Socrates was to recover that firm foundation for human life, which a misuse of the new intellectual spirit was rendering impossible. He effected much more for after times, and for the world, than for his own people. His amount of success with Alcibiades may probably be taken as giving us, well enough, the measure of his success with the Athenian people at large. 'As to the susceptibility of Alcibiades,' we are told, 'Socrates had not come too late, for he still found in him a youthful soul, susceptible of high inspirations. But to effect in him a permanent reaction, and a lasting and fixed change of mind, was beyond the power even of a Socrates.' Alcibiades oscillated and fell away; and the Athenian people, too, and Hellas as a whole, oscillated and fell away.

So it came to pass, that after Æschylus had sadly raised his voice to deprecate 'unblessed freedom from restraint,' and after complaints had been heard, again and again, of the loss of 'the ancient morality and piety,' of 'the old elements of Hellas, reflexion and moderation, discipline and social morality,' it came to pass that finally, at the end of the Peloponnesian war, 'one result,' the historian tells us, 'one result alone admitted of no doubt; and that was, the horribly rapid progress of the demoralisation of the Hellenic nation.'

Years and centuries rolled on, and, first, the Hellenic genius issued forth invading and vanquishing with Alexander; and then, when Rome had afterwards conquered Greece, conquered the conquerors, and overspread the civilised world. And still, joined to all the gifts and graces which that admirable genius brought with it, there went, as a kind of fatal accompaniment, moral inadequacy. And if one asked why

this was so, it seemed as if it could only be because the power of seriousness, of tenacious grasp upon grave and moral ideas, was wanting. And this again seemed as if it could only have for its cause, that these Hellenic natures were, in respect of their impressionability, mobility, flexibility, under the spell of a graceful but dangerous fairy, who would not let it be otherwise. 'Lest thou shouldst ponder the path of life,' says the Wise Man, '*her ways are moveable, that thou canst not know them.*' Then the new and reforming spirit, the Christian
10 spirit, which was rising in the world, turned sternly upon this gracious flexibility, changed the sense of its name, branded it with infamy, and classed it, along with 'filthiness and foolish talking,' among 'things which are not convenient.'

Now, there you see the historical course of our words *eutrapelos, eutrapelia,* and a specimen of the range, backwards and forwards, which a single phrase in one of our Greek or Latin classics may have.

And I might go yet further, and might show you, in the mediæval world, *eutrapelia,* or flexibility, quite banished,
20 clear straightforward Attic thinking quite lost; restraint, stoppage, and prejudice, regnant. And coming down to our own times, I might show you fearless thinking and flexibility once more, after many vicissitudes, coming into honour ; and again, perhaps, not without their accompaniment of danger. And the moral from all this,—apart from the particular moral that in our classical studies we may everywhere find clues which will lead us a long way,—the moral is, not that flexibility is a bad thing, but that the Greek flexibility was really not flexible enough, because it could not enough bend
30 itself to the moral ideas which are so large a part of life. Here, I say, is the true moral: that man has to make progress along diverse lines, in obedience to a diversity of aspirations and powers, the sum of which is truly his nature ; and that he fails and falls short until he learns to advance upon them all, and to advance upon them harmoniously.

Yes, this is the moral, and we all need it, and no nation more than ours. We so easily think that life is all on one line! Our nation, for instance, is above all things a political nation, and is apt to make far too much of politics. Many of us,—though not so very many, I suppose, of you here,—are Liberals, and think that to be a Liberal is quite enough for a man. Probably most of you here will have no difficulty in believing that to be a Liberal is not alone enough for a man, is not saving. One might even take,—and with your notions it would probably be a great treat for you,—one might take the last century of Athens, the century preceding the 'dishonest victory' of the Macedonian power, and show you a society dying of the triumph of the Liberal party. And then, again, as the young are generous, you might like to give the discomfited Liberals a respite, to let the other side have its turn ; and you might consent to be shown, as you could be shown in the age of Trajan and of the Antonines, a society dying of the triumph of the Conservative party. They were excellent people, the Conservative Roman aristocracy of that epoch ;—excellent, most respectable people, like the Conservatives of our own acquaintance. Only Conservatism, like Liberalism, taken alone, is not sufficient, is not of itself saving.

But you have had enough for one evening. And besides, the tendencies of the present day in education being what they are, before you proceed to hear more of this sort of thing, you ought certainly to be favoured, for several months to come, with a great many scientific lectures, and to busy yourselves considerably with the diameter of the sun and moon.

CIVILISATION

1861. *Mixed Essays* (1879)

CIVILISATION is the humanisation of man in society. Man is civilised, when the whole body of society comes to live with a life worthy to be called *human*, and corresponding to man's true aspirations and powers. The means by which man is brought towards this goal of his endeavour are various. It is of great importance to us to attain an adequate notion of them, and to keep it present before our minds. They may be conceived quite plainly, and enounced without any parade of hard and abstruse expression.

First and foremost of the necessary means towards man's civilisation we must name *expansion*. The need of expansion is as genuine an instinct in man as the need in plants for the
10 light, or the need in man himself for going upright. All the conveniences of life by which man has enlarged and secured his existence—railroads and the penny post among the number—are due to the working in man of this force or instinct of expansion. But the manifestation of it which we English know best, and prize most, is the love of liberty.

The love of liberty is simply the instinct in man for expansion. Not only to find oneself tyrannised over and outraged is a defeat to this instinct; but, in general, to feel oneself over-tutored, over-governed, *sate upon* (as the popular
20 phrase is) by authority, is a defeat to it. Prince Bismarck says: 'After all, a benevolent rational absolutism is the best form of government.' Plenty of arguments may be adduced in support of such a thesis. The one fatal objection to it is that it is against nature, that it contradicts a vital instinct in man—the instinct of expansion. And man is not to be civilised or humanised, call it which you will, by thwarting his vital instincts. In fact, the benevolent rational absolutism always breaks down. It is found that the ruler cannot in the long run be trusted; it is found that the ruled deterio-
30 rate. Why? Because the proceeding is against nature.

The other great manifestation of the instinct of expansion is the love of equality. Of the love of equality we English have little; but, undoubtedly, it is no more a false tendency than the love of liberty. Undoubtedly, immense inequality of conditions and property is a defeat to the instinct of ex-

growth of personality

pansion; it depresses and degrades the inferior masses. The
common people is and must be, as Tocqueville said, more
uncivilised in aristocratic countries than in any others. A
thousand arguments may be discovered in favour of inequality, just as a thousand arguments may be discovered in
favour of absolutism. And the one insuperable objection to
inequality is the same as the one insuperable objection to
absolutism: namely, that inequality, like absolutism, thwarts
a vital instinct, and being thus against nature, is against our
humanisation. On the one side, in fact, inequality harms by 10
pampering; on the other, by vulgarising and depressing. A
system founded on it is against nature, and in the long run
breaks down.

I put first among the elements in human civilisation the
instinct of expansion, because it is the basis which man's
whole effort to civilise himself presupposes. General civilisation presupposes this instinct, which is inseparable from
human nature; presupposes its being satisfied, not defeated.
The basis being given, we may rapidly enumerate the powers
which, upon this basis, contribute to build up human civilisa- 20
tion. They are the power of conduct, the power of intellect
and knowledge, the power of beauty, the power of social life
and manners. Expansion, conduct, science, beauty, manners,—here are the conditions of civilisation, the claimants
which man must satisfy before he can be humanised.

knowledge

ATHENS AND ISRAEL

1878. *Mixed Essays* (1879)

WHEN we talk of man's advance towards his full humanity,
we think of an advance, not along one line only, but several.
Certain races and nations, as we know, are on certain lines
pre-eminent and representative. The Hebrew nation was
pre-eminent on one great line. 'What nation,' it was justly 30
asked by their lawgiver, 'hath statutes and judgments so

righteous as the law which I set before you this day? Keep therefore and do them; for this is your wisdom and your understanding in the sight of the nations which shall hear all these statutes and say: Surely this great nation is a wise and understanding people!' The Hellenic race was pre-eminent on other lines. Isocrates could say of Athens: 'Our city has left the rest of the world so far behind in philosophy and eloquence, that those educated by Athens have become the teachers of the rest of mankind; and so well has she done
10 her part, that the name of Greeks seems no longer to stand for a race but to stand for intelligence itself, and they who share in our culture are called Greeks even before those who are merely of our own blood.' The power of intellect and science, the power of beauty, the power of social life and manners,—these are what Greece so felt, and fixed, and may stand for. They are great elements in our humanisation. The power of conduct is another great element; and this was so felt and fixed by Israel that we can never with justice refuse to permit Israel, in spite of all his shortcomings, to
20 stand for it.

RELIGION

1871. *Literature and Dogma* (1873)

Is there no difference between what is ethical, or morality, and religion? There *is* a difference; a difference of degree. Religion, if we allow the intention of human thought and human language in the use of the word, is ethics heightened, enkindled, lit up by feeling; the passage from morality to religion is made when to morality is applied emotion. And the true meaning of religion is thus, not simply *morality*, but *morality touched by emotion.* And this new elevation and inspiration of morality is well marked by the word 'righteous-
30 ness.' Conduct is the word of common life, morality is the word of philosophical disquisition, righteousness is the word of religion.

ASELGEIA

1884. *Discourses in America* (1885)

THE saints admonish us to let our thoughts run upon what-
soever things are pure, if we would inherit the kingdom of
God; and the divine Plato tells us that we have within us a
many-headed beast and a man, and that by dissoluteness we
feed and strengthen the beast in us, and starve the man; and
finally, following the divine Plato among the sages at a
humble distance, comes the prosaic and unfashionable Paley,
and says in his precise way that 'this vice has a tendency,
which other species of vice have not so directly, to unsettle
and weaken the powers of the understanding; as well as, I 10
think, in a greater degree than other vices, to render the
heart thoroughly corrupt.' True; and once admitted and
fostered, it eats like a canker, and with difficulty can ever
be brought to let go its hold again, but for ever tightens it.
Hardness and insolence come in its train; an insolence which
grows until it ends by exasperating and alienating every-
body; a hardness which grows until the man can at last
scarcely take pleasure in anything, outside the service of his
goddess, except cupidity and greed, and cannot be touched
with emotion by any language except fustian. Such are the 20
fruits of the worship of the great goddess Aselgeia.

PHILISTINES

1863. *Essays in Criticism* (1865)

PHILISTINISM!—We have not the expression in English.
Perhaps we have not the word because we have so much of
the thing. . . . In truth, the English, profoundly as they have
modified the old Middle-age order, great as is the liberty
which they have secured for themselves, have in all their
changes proceeded, to use a familiar expression, by the rule
of thumb; what was intolerably inconvenient to them they

have suppressed, and as they have suppressed it, not because it was irrational, but because it was practically inconvenient, they have seldom in suppressing it appealed to
reason, but always, if possible, to some precedent, or form,
or letter, which served as a convenient instrument for their
purpose, and which saved them from the necessity of recur-
ring to general principles. They have thus become, in a
certain sense, of all people the most inaccessible to ideas and
the most impatient of them; inaccessible to them, because
10 of their want of familiarity with them; and impatient of
them because they have got on so well without them, that
they despise those who, not having got on as well as themselves, still make a fuss for what they themselves have done
so well without. But there has certainly followed from hence,
in this country, somewhat of a general depression of pure
intelligence: Philistia has come to be thought by us the true
Land of Promise, and it is anything but that; the born lover
of ideas, the born hater of commonplaces, must feel in this
country, that the sky over his head is of brass and iron. The
20 enthusiast for the idea, for reason, values reason, the idea,
in and for themselves; he values them, irrespectively of the
practical conveniences which their triumph may obtain for
him; and the man who regards the possession of those practical conveniences as something sufficient in itself, something
which compensates for the absence or surrender of the idea,
of reason, is, in his eyes, a Philistine.

BARBARIANS

1868. *Culture and Anarchy* (1869)

I HAVE in my own mind often indulged myself with the fancy
of employing, in order to designate our aristocratic class, the
name of *The Barbarians*. The Barbarians, to whom we all
30 owe so much, and who reinvigorated and renewed our worn-
out Europe, had, as is well known, eminent merits; and in

this country, where we are for the most part sprung from the Barbarians, we have never had the prejudice against them which prevails among the races of Latin origin. The Barbarians brought with them that staunch individualism, as the modern phrase is, and that passion for doing as one likes, for the assertion of personal liberty, which appears to Mr. Bright the central idea of English life, and of which we have, at any rate, a very rich supply. The stronghold and natural seat of this passion was in the nobles of whom our aristocratic class are the inheritors; and this class, accordingly, have signally 10 manifested it, and have done much by their example to recommend it to the body of the nation, who already, indeed, had it in their blood. The Barbarians, again, had the passion for field-sports; and they have handed it on to our aristocratic class, who of this passion too, as of the passion for asserting one's personal liberty, are the great natural stronghold. The care of the Barbarians for the body, and for all manly exercises; the vigour, good looks, and fine complexion which they acquired and perpetuated in their families by these means,—all this may be observed still in our aristo- 20 cratic class. The chivalry of the Barbarians, with its characteristics of high spirit, choice manners, and distinguished bearing,—what is this but the attractive commencement of the politeness of our aristocratic class? In some Barbarian noble, no doubt, one would have admired, if one could have been then alive to see it, the rudiments of our politest peer. Only, all this culture (to call it by that name) of the Barbarians was an exterior culture mainly. It consisted principally in outward gifts and graces, in looks, manners, accomplishments, prowess. The chief inward gifts which had part in it 30 were the most exterior, so to speak, of inward gifts, those which come nearest to outward ones; they were courage, a high spirit, self-confidence. Far within, and unawakened, lay a whole range of powers of thought and feeling, to which these interesting productions of nature had, from the

L

circumstances of their life, no access. Making allowances for the difference of the times, surely we can observe precisely the same thing now in our aristocratic class. In general its culture is exterior chiefly; all the exterior graces and accomplishments, and the more external of the inward virtues, seem to be principally its portion. It now, of course, cannot but be often in contact with those studies by which, from the world of thought and feeling, true culture teaches us to fetch sweetness and light; but its hold upon these very studies appears remarkably external, and unable to exert any deep power upon its spirit. Therefore the one insufficiency which we noted in the perfect mean of this class was an insufficiency of light. And owing to the same causes, does not a subtle criticism lead us to make, even on the good looks and politeness of our aristocratic class, and of even the most fascinating half of that class, the feminine half, the one qualifying remark, that in these charming gifts there should perhaps be, for ideal perfection, a shade more *soul*?

I often, therefore, when I want to distinguish clearly the aristocratic class from the Philistines proper, or middle class, name the former, in my own mind, *The Barbarians*. And when I go through the country, and see this and that beautiful and imposing seat of theirs crowning the landscape, 'There,' I say to myself, 'is a great fortified post of the Barbarians.'

CULTURE

1867. *Culture and Anarchy* (1869)

THE disparagers of culture make its motive curiosity; sometimes, indeed, they make its motive mere exclusiveness and vanity. The culture which is supposed to plume itself on a smattering of Greek and Latin is a culture which is begotten by nothing so intellectual as curiosity; it is valued either out of sheer vanity and ignorance, or else as an engine of social and class distinction, separating its holder, like a badge or title, from other people who have not got it. No serious man would call this *culture*, or attach any value to it, as culture, at all. . . . There is certainly a curiosity,—a desire after the things of the mind simply for their own sakes and for the pleasure of seeing them as they are,—which is, in an intelligent being, natural and laudable. Nay, and the very desire to see things as they are, implies a balance and regulation of mind which is not often attained without fruitful effort, and which is the very opposite of the blind and diseased impulse of mind which is what we mean to blame when we blame curiosity. Montesquieu says:—'The first motive which ought to impel us to study is the desire to augment the excellence of our nature, and to render an intelligent being yet more intelligent.' This is the true ground to assign for the genuine scientific passion, however manifested, and for culture, viewed simply as a fruit of this passion; and it is a worthy ground, even though we let the term *curiosity* stand to describe it.

But there is of culture another view, in which not solely the scientific passion, the sheer desire to see things as they are, natural and proper in an intelligent being, appears as the ground of it. There is a view in which all the love of our neighbour, the impulses towards action, help, and beneficence, the desire for removing human error, clearing human confusion, and diminishing human misery, the noble aspiration to leave the world better and happier than we found it, —motives eminently such as are called social,—come in as part of the grounds of culture, and the main and pre-eminent part. Culture is then properly described not as having its origin in curiosity, but as having its origin in the love of perfection; it is *a study of perfection*. It moves by the force, not merely or primarily of the scientific passion for pure knowledge, but also of the moral and social passion for doing good. As, in the first view of it, we took for its worthy motto

Montesquieu's words: 'To render an intelligent being yet more intelligent!' so, in the second view of it, there is no better motto which it can have than these words of Bishop Wilson: 'To make reason and the will of God prevail!'

SWEETNESS AND LIGHT

1867. *Culture and Anarchy* (1869)

THE Greek word εὐφυΐα, a finely tempered nature, gives exactly the notion of perfection as culture brings us to conceive it: a harmonious perfection, a perfection in which the characters of beauty and intelligence are both present, which unites 'the two noblest of things,'—as Swift, who of one of
10 the two, at any rate, had himself all too little, most happily calls them in his *Battle of the Books*,—'the two noblest of things, *sweetness and light*.' The εὐφυής is the man who tends towards sweetness and light; the ἀφυής, on the other hand, is our Philistine. The immense spiritual significance of the Greeks is due to their having been inspired with this central and happy idea of the essential character of human perfection.

POETRY A CRITICISM OF LIFE

1879. *Essays in Criticism* (1888)

IT is important to hold fast to this: that poetry is at bottom a criticism of life; that the greatness of a poet lies in his
20 powerful and beautiful application of ideas to life,—to the question: How to live? Morals are often treated in a narrow and false fashion ; they are bound up with systems of thought and belief which have had their day ; they are fallen into the hands of pedants and professional dealers ; they grow tiresome to some of us. We find attraction, at times, even in a poetry of revolt against them ; in a poetry which might take for its motto Omar Kheyam's words: 'Let us make up in the

tavern for the time which we have wasted in the mosque.'
Or we find attractions in a poetry indifferent to them; in a
poetry where the contents may be what they will, but where
the form is studied and exquisite. We delude ourselves in
either case; and the best cure for our delusion is to let our
minds rest upon that great and inexhaustible word *life*, until
we learn to enter into its meaning. A poetry of revolt against
moral ideas is a poetry of revolt against *life*; a poetry of
indifference towards moral ideas is a poetry of indifference
towards *life*.   10

THE BEST POETRY

1880. *Essays in Criticism* (1888)

WE should conceive of poetry worthily, and more highly
than it has been the custom to conceive of it. We should
conceive of it as capable of higher uses, and called to higher
destinies, than those which in general men have assigned to
it hitherto. More and more mankind will discover that we
have to turn to poetry to interpret life for us, to console us,
to sustain us. Without poetry, our science will appear incomplete; and most of what now passes with us for religion
and philosophy will be replaced by poetry. Science, I say,
will appear incomplete without it. For finely and truly does 20
Wordsworth call poetry 'the impassioned expression which
is in the countenance of all science'; and what is a countenance without its expression? Again, Wordsworth finely
and truly calls poetry 'the breath and finer spirit of all knowledge': our religion, parading evidences such as those on
which the popular mind relies now; our philosophy, pluming
itself on its reasonings about causation and finite and infinite
being; what are they but the shadows and dreams and false
shows of knowledge? The day will come when we shall
wonder at ourselves for having trusted to them, for having 30

taken them seriously; and the more we perceive their hol-
lowness, the more we shall prize 'the breath and finer spirit
of knowledge' offered to us by poetry.

But if we conceive thus highly of the destinies of poetry, we
must also set our standard for poetry high, since poetry, to
be capable of fulfilling such high destinies, must be poetry
of a high order of excellence. We must accustom ourselves
to a high standard and to a strict judgment. Sainte-Beuve
relates that Napoleon one day said, when somebody was
10 spoken of in his presence as a charlatan: 'Charlatan as much
as you please; but where is there *not* charlatanism?'—'Yes,'
answers Sainte-Beuve, 'in politics, in the art of governing
mankind, that is perhaps true. But in the order of thought,
in art, the glory, the eternal honour is that charlatanism
shall find no entrance; herein lies the inviolableness of that
noble portion of man's being.' It is admirably said, and let
us hold fast to it. In poetry, which is thought and art in one,
it is the glory, the eternal honour, that charlatanism shall
find no entrance; that this noble sphere be kept inviolate
20 and inviolable. Charlatanism is for confusing or obliterating
the distinctions between excellent and inferior, sound and
unsound or only half-sound, true and untrue or only half-
true. It is charlatanism, conscious or unconscious whenever
we confuse or obliterate these. And in poetry, more than
anywhere else, it is unpermissible to confuse or obliterate
them. For in poetry the distinction between excellent and
inferior, sound and unsound or only half-sound, true and
untrue or only half-true, is of paramount importance. It is
of paramount importance because of the high destinies of
30 poetry. In poetry, as a criticism of life under the conditions
fixed for such a criticism by the laws of poetic truth and
poetic beauty, the spirit of our race will find, we have said,
as time goes on and as other helps fail, its consolation and
stay. But the consolation and stay will be of power in proportion to the power of the criticism of life. And the criti-

cism of life will be of power in proportion as the poetry
conveying it is excellent rather than inferior, sound rather
than unsound or half-sound, true rather than untrue or half-
true. The best poetry is what we want; the best poetry will
be found to have a power of forming, sustaining, and delighting us, as nothing else can.

HOW POETRY INTERPRETS

1863. *Essays in Criticism* (1865)

THE grand power of poetry is its interpretative power; by
which I mean, not a power of drawing out in black and
white an explanation of the mystery of the universe, but the
power of so dealing with things as to awaken in us a wonder- 10
fully full, new, and intimate sense of them, and of our relations with them. When this sense is awakened in us, as to
objects without us, we feel ourselves to be in contact with
the essential nature of those objects, to be no longer be-
wildered and oppressed by them, but to have their secret,
and to be in harmony with them; and this feeling calms and
satisfies us as no other can. Poetry, indeed, interprets in
another way besides this; but one of its two ways of inter-
preting, of exercising its highest power, is by awaking this
sense in us. I will not now inquire whether this sense is 20
illusive, whether it can be proved not to be illusive, whether
it does absolutely make us possess the real nature of things;
all I say is, that poetry can awaken it in us, and that to
awaken it is one of the highest powers of poetry. The interpretations of science do not give us this intimate sense of
objects as the interpretations of poetry give it; they appeal
to a limited faculty, and not to the whole man. It is not
Linnaeus, or Cavendish, or Cuvier who gives us the true
sense of animals, or water, or plants, who seizes their secret

for us, who makes us participate in their life; it is Shak-speare, with his

> 'daffodils
> That come before the swallow dares, and take
> The winds of March with beauty;'

it is Wordsworth, with his

> 'voice . . . heard
> In spring-time from the cuckoo-bird,
> Breaking the silence of the seas
> Among the farthest Hebrides;'

it is Keats with his

> 'moving waters at their priestlike task
> Of cold ablution round Earth's human shores. . . .'

I have said that poetry interprets in two ways; it inter-prets by expressing with magical felicity the physiognomy and movement of the outward world, and it interprets by expressing with inspired conviction the ideas and laws of the inward world of man's moral and spiritual nature. In other words, poetry is interpretative both by having *natural magic* in it, and by having *moral profundity*. In both ways it illumi-nates man; it gives to him a satisfying sense of reality; it reconciles him with himself and the universe. Thus Æschy-lus's '$\delta\rho\acute{a}\sigma\alpha\nu\tau\iota\ \pi\alpha\theta\epsilon\hat{\iota}\nu$' and his '$\dot{a}\nu\acute{\eta}\rho\iota\theta\mu o\nu\ \gamma\acute{\epsilon}\lambda\alpha\sigma\mu\alpha$' are alike interpretative. Shakspeare interprets both when he says:

> Full many a glorious morning have I seen,
> Flatter the mountain-tops with sovran eye;

and when he says:

> There's a divinity that shapes our ends,
> Rough-hew them as we will.

These great poets unite in themselves the faculty of both kinds of interpretation, the naturalistic and the moral. But it is observable that in the poets who unite both kinds, the latter (the moral) usually ends by making itself the master.

NATURAL MAGIC

1866. *The Study of Celtic Literature* (1867)

THE Celt's quick feeling for what is noble and distinguished gave to his poetry style; his indomitable personality gave it pride and passion; his sensibility and nervous exaltation gave it a better gift still, the gift of rendering with wonderful felicity the magical charm of nature. The forest solitude, the bubbling spring, the wild flowers, are everywhere in romance. They have a mysterious life and grace there; they are nature's own children, and utter her secret in a way which makes them something quite different from the woods, waters, and plants of Greek and Latin poetry. Now, of this delicate 10 natural magic Celtic romance is so pre-eminent a mistress, that it seems impossible to believe the power did not come into romance from the Celts. Magic is just the word for it— the magic of nature; not merely the beauty of nature,—that the Greeks and Latins had; not merely an honest smack of the soil, a faithful realism,—that the Germans had; but the intimate life of nature, her weird power and her fairy charm. As the Saxon names of places, with the pleasant wholesome smack of the soil in them,—Weathersfield, Thaxted, Shal-ford,—are to the Celtic names of places, with their penetrat- 20 ing, lofty beauty,—Velindra, Tyntagel, Caernarvon,—so is the homely realism of German and Norse nature to the fairy-like loveliness of Celtic nature. Gwydion wants a wife for his pupil: 'Well,' says Math, 'we will seek, I and thou, by charms and illusions, to form a wife for him out of flowers. So they took the blossoms of the oak, and the blossoms of the broom, and the blossoms of the meadow-sweet, and produced from them a maiden, the fairest and most graceful that man ever saw. And they baptised her, and gave her the name of Flower-Aspect.' Celtic romance is full of exquisite touches 30 like that, showing the delicacy of the Celt's feeling in these matters, and how deeply nature lets him come into her secrets.

DISINTERESTEDNESS IN CRITICISM

1864. *Essays in Criticism* (1865)

IT is of the last importance that English criticism should
clearly discern what rule for its course, in order to avail
itself of the field now opening to it, and to produce fruit for
the future, it ought to take. The rule may be summed up
in one word,—*disinterestedness*. And how is criticism to
show disinterestedness? By keeping aloof from what is
called 'the practical view of things'; by resolutely following
the law of its own nature, which is to be a free play of the
mind on all subjects which it touches. By steadily refusing
10 to lend itself to any of those ulterior, political, practical
considerations about ideas, which plenty of people will be
sure to attach to them, which perhaps ought often to be
attached to them, which in this country at any rate are
certain to be attached to them quite sufficiently, but which
criticism has really nothing to do with. Its business is, as
I have said, simply to know the best that is known and
thought in the world, and by in its turn making this known,
to create a current of true and fresh ideas. Its business is to
do this with inflexible honesty, with due ability; but its
20 business is to do no more, and to leave alone all questions
of practical consequences and applications, questions which
will never fail to have due prominence given to them.

OXFORD

Essays in Criticism (1865)

BEAUTIFUL city,—so venerable, so lovely, so unravaged by
the fierce intellectual life of our century, so serene!

There are our young barbarians, all at play!

And yet, steeped in sentiment as she lies, spreading her gardens to the moonlight, and whispering from her towers the

last enchantments of the Middle Age, who will deny that
Oxford, by her ineffable charm, keeps ever calling us nearer
to the true goal of all of us, to the ideal, to perfection,—to
beauty, in a word, which is only truth seen from another side?
—nearer, perhaps, than all the science of Tübingen. Adorable
dreamer, whose heart has been so romantic! who hast given
thyself so prodigally, given thyself to sides and to heroes not
mine, only never to the Philistines! home of lost causes, and
forsaken beliefs, and unpopular names, and impossible loyal-
ties! what example could ever so inspire us to keep down the 10
Philistine in ourselves, what teacher could ever so save us
from that bondage to which we are all prone, that bondage
which Goethe, in his incomparable lines on the death of
Schiller, makes it his friend's highest praise (and nobly did
Schiller deserve the praise) to have left miles out of sight
behind him;—the bondage of *was uns alle bändigt, DAS
GEMEINE!*' Oxford will forgive me, even if I have unwit-
tingly drawn upon her a shot or two aimed at her unworthy
son; for she is generous, and the cause in which I fight is,
after all, hers. Apparitions of a day, what is our puny war- 20
fare against the Philistines, compared with the warfare which
this queen of romance has been waging against them for
centuries, and will wage after we are gone?

CHAUCER

1880. *Essays in Criticism* (1888)

IF we ask ourselves wherein consists the immense superiority
of Chaucer's poetry over the romance-poetry—why it is that
in passing from this to Chaucer we suddenly feel ourselves
to be in another world, we shall find that his superiority is
both in the substance of his poetry and in the style of his
poetry. His superiority in substance is given by his large, free,
simple, clear yet kindly view of human life,—so unlike the 30
total want, in the romance-poets, of all intelligent command

of it. Chaucer has not their helplessness; he has gained the
power to survey the world from a central, a truly human
point of view. We have only to call to mind the Prologue to
The Canterbury Tales. The right comment upon it is Dryden's: 'It is sufficient to say, according to the proverb, that
here is God's plenty.' And again: 'He is a perpetual fountain
of good sense.' It is by a large, free, sound representa-
tion of things, that poetry, this high criticism of life, has truth
of substance: and Chaucer's poetry has truth of substance.
10   Of his style and manner, if we think first of the romance-
poetry and then of Chaucer's divine liquidness of diction, his
divine fluidity of movement, it is difficult to speak temper-
ately. They are irresistible, and justify all the rapture with
which his successors speak of his 'gold dew-drops of speech.'
Johnson misses the point entirely when he finds fault with
Dryden for ascribing to Chaucer the first refinement of our
numbers, and says that Gower also can show smooth numbers and easy rhymes. The refinement of our numbers means
something far more than this. A nation may have versifiers
20 with smooth numbers and easy rhymes, and yet may have
no real poetry at all. Chaucer is the father of our splendid
English poetry; he is our 'well of English undefiled,' because
by the lovely charm of his diction, the lovely charm of his
movement, he makes an epoch and founds a tradition. In
Spenser, Shakespeare, Milton, Keats, we can follow the
tradition of the liquid diction, the fluid movement, of
Chaucer; at one time it is his liquid diction of which in these
poets we feel the virtue, and at another time it is his fluid
movement. And the virtue is irresistible. . . .
30   And yet Chaucer is not one of the great classics. His
poetry transcends and effaces, easily and without effort, all
the romance-poetry of Catholic Christendom; it transcends
and effaces all the English poetry contemporary with it; it
transcends and effaces all the English poetry subsequent to
it down to the age of Elizabeth. Of such avail is poetic truth

of substance, in its natural and necessary union with poetic truth of style. And yet, I say, Chaucer is not one of the great classics. He has not their accent. What is wanting to him is suggested by the mere mention of the name of the first great classic of Christendom, the immortal poet who died eighty years before Chaucer,—Dante. The accent of such verse as

'In la sua volontade è nostra pace . . .'

is altogether beyond Chaucer's reach; we praise him, but we feel that this accent is out of the question for him. 10 It may be said that it was necessarily out of the reach of any poet in the England of that stage of growth. Possibly; but we are to adopt a real, not a historic, estimate of poetry. However we may account for its absence, something is wanting, then, to the poetry of Chaucer, which poetry must have before it can be placed in the glorious class of the best. And there is no doubt what that something is. It is the σπουδαιότης, the high and excellent seriousness, which Aristotle assigns as one of the grand virtues of poetry. The substance of Chaucer's poetry, his view of things and his 20 criticism of life, has largeness, freedom, shrewdness, benignity; but it has not this high seriousness. Homer's criticism of life has it, Dante's has it, Shakespeare's has it. It is this chiefly which gives to our spirits what they can rest upon; and with the increasing demands of our modern ages upon poetry, this virtue of giving us what we can rest upon will be more and more highly esteemed.

SHAKESPEARE

1853. *Irish Essays* (1882)

FOREMOST among the models for the English writer stands Shakespeare: a name the greatest perhaps of all poetical names; a name never to be mentioned without reverence. 30 I will venture, however, to express a doubt, whether the

influence of his works, excellent and fruitful for the readers
of poetry, for the great majority, has been of unmixed
advantage to the writers of it. Shakespeare indeed chose
excellent subjects; the world could afford no better than
Macbeth, or Romeo and Juliet, or Othello; he had no theory
respecting the necessity of choosing subjects of present im-
port, or the paramount interest attaching to allegories of
the state of one's own mind; like all great poets, he knew
well what constituted a poetical action; like them, wherever
10 he found such an action, he took it; like them, too, he found
his best in past times. But to these general characteristics
of all great poets he added a special one of his own; a gift,
namely, of happy, abundant, and ingenious expression,
eminent and unrivalled: so eminent as irresistibly to strike
the attention first in him, and even to throw into compara-
tive shade his other excellences as a poet. Here has been the
mischief. These other excellences were his fundamental
excellences *as a poet*; what distinguishes the artist from the
mere amateur, says Goethe, is *Architectonicè* in the highest
20 sense; that power of execution, which creates, forms, and
constitutes: not the profoundness of single thoughts, not the
richness of imagery, not the abundance of illustration. But
these attractive accessories of a poetical work being more
easily seized than the spirit of the whole, and these accessories being possessed by Shakespeare in an unequalled
degree, a young writer having recourse to Shakespeare as
his model runs great risk of being vanquished and absorbed
by them, and, in consequence, of reproducing, according to
the measure of his power, these, and these alone. Of this
30 preponderating quality of Shakespeare's genius, accordingly,
almost the whole of modern English poetry has, it appears to
me, felt the influence.

MILTON

1878. *Mixed Essays* (1879)

MILTON's true distinction as a poet is undoubtedly his 'un-failing level of style.' Milton has always the sure, strong touch of the master. His power both of diction and of rhythm is unsurpassable, and it is characterised by being always present;—not depending on an access of emotion, not intermittent, but, like the grace of Raphael, working in its possessor as a constant gift of nature. Milton's style, moreover, has the same propriety and soundness in pre-senting plain matters, as in the comparatively smooth task for a poet of presenting grand ones. His rhythm is as 10 admirable where, as in the line

And Tiresias and Phineus, prophets old——

it is unusual, as in such lines as—

With dreadful faces throng'd and fiery arms——

where it is simplest. And what high praise this is, we may best appreciate by considering the ever-recurring failure, both in rhythm and in diction, which we find in the so-called Miltonic blank verse of Thomson, Cowper, Wordsworth. What leagues of lumbering movement! what desperate en-deavours, as in Wordsworth's 20

And at the 'Hoop' alighted, famous inn,

to render a platitude endurable by making it pompous! Shakspeare himself, divine as are his gifts, has not, of the marks of the master, this one: perfect sureness of hand in his style. Alone of English poets, alone in English art, Milton has it; he is our great artist in style, our one first-rate master in the grand style.

WORDSWORTH

1879. *Essays in Criticism* (1888)

WORDSWORTH'S poetry is great because of the extraordinary power with which Wordsworth feels the joy offered to us in nature, the joy offered to us in the simple primary affections and duties; and because of the extraordinary power with which, in case after case, he shows us this joy, and renders it so as to make us share it.

The source of joy from which he thus draws is the truest and most unfailing source of joy accessible to man. It is also accessible universally. Wordsworth brings us word, there-
10 fore, according to his own strong and characteristic line, he brings us word

'Of joy in widest commonalty spread.'

Here is an immense advantage for a poet. Wordsworth tells of what all seek, and tells of it at its truest and best source, and yet a source where all may go and draw for it.

Nevertheless, we are not to suppose that everything is precious which Wordsworth, standing even at this perennial and beautiful source, may give us. Wordsworthians are apt to talk as if it must be. They will speak with the same
20 reverence of *The Sailor's Mother*, for example, as of *Lucy Gray*. They do their master harm by such lack of discrimination. *Lucy Gray* is a beautiful success; *The Sailor's Mother* is a failure. To give aright what he wishes to give, to interpret and render successfully, is not always within Wordsworth's own command. It is within no poet's command; here is the part of the Muse, the inspiration, the God, the 'not ourselves.' In Wordsworth's case, the accident, for so it may almost be called, of inspiration, is of peculiar importance. No poet, perhaps, is so evidently filled with a new
30 and sacred energy when the inspiration is upon him; no poet, when it fails him, is so left 'weak as is a breaking wave.'

I remember hearing him say that 'Goethe's poetry was not inevitable enough.' The remark is striking and true ; no line in Goethe, as Goethe said himself, but its maker knew well how it came there. Wordsworth is right, Goethe's poetry is not inevitable ; not inevitable enough. But Wordsworth's poetry, when he is at his best, is inevitable, as inevitable as Nature herself. It might seem that Nature not only gave him the matter for his poem, but wrote his poem for him. He has no style. He was too conversant with Milton not to catch at times his master's manner, and he has fine Miltonic lines ; but he has no assured poetic style of his own, like Milton. When he seeks to have a style he falls into ponderosity and pomposity. In the *Excursion* we have his style, as an artistic product of his own creation ; and although Jeffrey completely failed to recognise Wordsworth's real greatness, he was yet not wrong in saying of the *Excursion*, as a work of poetic style: 'This will never do.' And yet magical as is that power, which Wordsworth has not, of assured and possessed poetic style, he has something which is an equivalent for it.

Every one who has any sense for these things feels the subtle turn, the heightening, which is given to a poet's verse by his genius for style. We can feel it in the

'After life's fitful fever, he sleeps well'—

of Shakespeare ; in the

'. . . though fall'n on evil days,
On evil days though fall'n, and evil tongues'—

of Milton. It is the incomparable charm of Milton's power of poetic style which gives such worth to *Paradise Regained*, and makes a great poem of a work in which Milton's imagination does not soar high. Wordsworth has in constant possession, and at command, no style of this kind ; but he had too poetic a nature, and had read the great poets too well, not to catch, as I have already remarked, something of it occasion-

ally. We find it not only in his Miltonic lines; we find it in
such a phrase as this, where the manner is his own, not
Milton's—

> '. . . the fierce confederate storm
> Of sorrow barricadoed evermore
> Within the walls of cities;'

although even here, perhaps, the power of style which is
undeniable, is more properly that of eloquent prose than
the subtle heightening and change wrought by genuine
10 poetic style. It is style, again, and the elevation given by
style, which chiefly makes the effectiveness of *Laodamia*.
Still the right sort of verse to choose from Wordsworth, if
we are to seize his true and most characteristic form of
expression, is a line like this from *Michael*—

> 'And never lifted up a single stone.'

There is nothing subtle in it, no heightening, no study of
poetic style, strictly so called, at all; yet it is expression of
the highest and most truly expressive kind.

Wordsworth owed much to Burns, and a style of perfect
20 plainness, relying for effect solely on the weight and force
of that which with entire fidelity it utters, Burns could show
him.

> 'The poor inhabitant below
> Was quick to learn and wise to know,
> And keenly felt the friendly glow
>   And softer flame;
> But thoughtless follies laid him low
>   And stain'd his name.'

Every one will be conscious of a likeness here to Words-
30 worth; and if Wordsworth did great things with this nobly
plain manner, we must remember, what indeed he himself
would always have been forward to acknowledge, that Burns
used it before him.

Still Wordsworth's use of it has something unique and

unmatchable. Nature herself seems, I say, to take the pen out of his hand, and to write for him with her own bare, sheer, penetrating power. This arises from two causes; from the profound sincereness with which Wordsworth feels his subject, and also from the profoundly sincere and natural character of his subject itself. He can and will treat such a subject with nothing but the most plain, first-hand, almost austere naturalness. His expression may often be called bald, as, for instance, in the poem of *Resolution and Independence*; but it is bald as the bare mountain tops are bald, with a baldness which is full of grandeur. . . .

With the ancients I will not compare him. In many respects the ancients are far above us, and yet there is something that we demand which they can never give. Leaving the ancients, let us come to the poets and poetry of Christendom. Dante, Shakespeare, Molière, Milton, Goethe, are altogether larger and more splendid luminaries in the poetical heaven than Wordsworth. But I know not where else, among the moderns, we are to find his superiors.

COLERIDGE

1864. *Essays in Criticism* (1865)

COLERIDGE had less delicacy and penetration than Joubert, but more richness and power; his production, though far inferior to what his nature at first seemed to promise, was abundant and varied. Yet in all his production how much is there to dissatisfy us! How many reserves must be made in praising either his poetry, or his criticism, or his philosophy! How little either of his poetry, or of his criticism, or of his philosophy, can we expect permanently to stand! But that which will stand of Coleridge is this: the stimulus of his continual effort,—not a moral effort, for he had no morals,—but of his continual instinctive effort, crowned often with rich success, to get at and to lay bare the real

truth of his matter in hand, whether that matter were literary, or philosophical, or political, or religious; and this in a country where at that moment such an effort was almost unknown; where the most powerful minds threw themselves upon poetry, which conveys truth, indeed, but conveys it indirectly; and where ordinary minds were so habituated to do without thinking altogether, to regard considerations of established routine and practical convenience as paramount, that any attempt to introduce within the domain of these
10 the disturbing element of thought, they were prompt to resent as an outrage. Coleridge's great usefulness lay in his supplying in England, for many years and under critical circumstances, by the spectacle of this effort of his, a stimulus to all minds capable of profiting by it in the generation which grew up around him. His action will still be felt as long as the need for it continues. When, with the cessation of the need, the action too has ceased, Coleridge's memory, in spite of the disesteem,—nay, repugnance,—which his character may and must inspire, will yet for ever remain
20 invested with that interest and gratitude which invests the memory of founders.

BYRON

1881. *Essays in Criticism* (1888)

TRUE, as a man, Byron could not manage himself, could not guide his ways aright, but was all astray. True, he has no light, cannot lead us from the past to the future; 'the moment he reflects, he is a child.' The way out of the false state of things which enraged him he did not see,—the slow and laborious way upward; he had not the patience, knowledge, self-discipline, virtue, requisite for seeing it. True, also, as a poet, he has no fine and exact sense for word and
30 structure and rhythm; he has not the artist's nature and gifts. Yet a personality of Byron's force counts for so much in life, and a rhetorician of Byron's force counts for so much

in literature! But it would be most unjust to label Byron
as a rhetorician only. Along with his astounding power and
passion he had a strong and deep sense for what is beautiful
in nature, and for what is beautiful in human action and
suffering. When he warms to his work, when he is inspired,
Nature herself seems to take the pen from him as she took
it from Wordsworth, and to write for him as she wrote for
Wordsworth, though in a different fashion, with her own
penetrating simplicity. . . .

His own aristocratic class, whose cynical make-believe 10
drove him to fury; the great middle-class, on whose impreg-
nable Philistinism he shattered himself to pieces,—how little
have either of these felt Byron's vital influence! As the
inevitable break-up of the old order comes, as the English
middle-class slowly awakens from its intellectual sleep of
two centuries, as our actual present world, to which this
sleep has condemned us, shows itself more clearly,—our
world of an aristocracy materialised and null, a middle-class
purblind and hideous, a lower class crude and brutal,—we
shall turn our eyes again, and to more purpose, upon this 20
passionate and dauntless soldier of a forlorn hope, who,
ignorant of the future and unconsoled by its promises, nevertheless waged against the conservation of the old impossible
world so fiery battle; waged it till he fell,—waged it with
such splendid and imperishable excellence of sincerity and
strength.

Wordsworth's value is of another kind. Wordsworth has
an insight into permanent sources of joy and consolation for
mankind which Byron has not; his poetry gives us more
which we may rest upon than Byron's,—more which we can 30
rest upon now, and which men may rest upon always. I
place Wordsworth's poetry, therefore, above Byron's on the
whole, although in some points he was greatly Byron's inferior, and although Byron's poetry will always, probably,
find more readers than Wordsworth's, and will give pleasure

more easily. But these two, Wordsworth and Byron, stand,
it seems to me, first and pre-eminent in actual performance,
a glorious pair, among the English poets of this century.
Keats had probably, indeed, a more consummate poetic gift
than either of them; but he died having produced too little
and being as yet too immature to rival them. I for my part
can never even think of equalling with them any other
of their contemporaries;—either Coleridge, poet and philosopher wrecked in a mist of opium; or Shelley, beautiful and
10 ineffectual angel, beating in the void his luminous wings in
vain.

KEATS

1880. *Essays in Criticism* (1888)

THE truth is that 'the yearning passion for the Beautiful,'
which was with Keats, as he himself truly says, the master-
passion, is not a passion of the sensuous or sentimental man,
is not a passion of the sensuous or sentimental poet. It is
an intellectual and spiritual passion. It is 'connected and
made one,' as Keats declares that in his case it was, 'with
the ambition of the intellect.' It is, as he again says, 'the
mighty *abstract idea* of Beauty in all things.' And in his last
20 days Keats wrote: 'If I should die, I have left no immortal
work behind me—nothing to make my friends proud of my
memory; *but I have loved the principle of beauty in all things,*
and if I had had time I would have made myself remembered.' He *has* made himself remembered, and remembered
as no merely sensuous poet could be; and he has done it by
having 'loved the principle of beauty in all things.'

For to see things in their beauty is to see things in their
truth, and Keats knew it. 'What the Imagination seizes as
Beauty must be Truth,' he says in prose; and in immortal
30 verse he has said the same thing—

> 'Beauty is truth, truth beauty,—that is all
> Ye know on earth, and all ye need to know.'

No, it is not all; but it is true, deeply true, and we have deep need to know it. And with beauty goes not only truth, joy goes with her also; and this too Keats saw and said, as in the famous first line of his *Endymion* it stands written—

'A thing of beauty is a joy for ever.'

It is no small thing to have so loved the principle of beauty as to perceive the necessary relation of beauty with truth, and of both with joy. Keats was a great spirit, and counts for far more than many even of his admirers suppose, because this just and high perception made itself clear to him. Therefore a dignity and a glory shed gleams over his life, and happiness, too, was not a stranger to it. . . .

Let and hindered as he was, and with a short term and imperfect experience,—'young,' as he says of himself, 'and writing at random, straining after particles of light in the midst of a great darkness, without knowing the bearing of any one assertion, of any one opinion,'—notwithstanding all this, by virtue of his feeling for beauty and of his perception of the vital connection of beauty with truth, Keats accomplished so much in poetry, that in one of the two great modes by which poetry interprets, in the faculty of naturalistic interpretation, in what we call natural magic, he ranks with Shakespeare. 'The tongue of Kean,' he says in an admirable criticism of that great actor and of his enchanting elocution, 'the tongue of Kean must seem to have robbed the Hybla bees and left them honeyless. There is an indescribable *gusto* in his voice;—in *Richard*, "Be stirring with the lark to-morrow, gentle Norfolk!" comes from him as through the morning atmosphere towards which he yearns'. This magic, this 'indescribable *gusto* in the voice,' Keats himself, too, exhibits in his poetic expression. No one else in English poetry, save Shakespeare, has in expression quite the fascinating felicity of Keats, his perfection of loveliness. I think,' he said humbly, 'I shall be among the English poets after my death.' He is; he is with Shakespeare.

For the second great half of poetic interpretation, for that faculty of moral interpretation which is in Shakespeare, and is informed by him with the same power of beauty as his naturalistic interpretation, Keats was not ripe. For the architectonics of poetry, the faculty which presides at the evolution of works like the *Agamemnon* or *Lear*, he was not ripe. His *Endymion*, as he himself well saw, is a failure, and
10 his *Hyperion*, fine things as it contains, is not a success. But in shorter things, where the matured power of moral interpretation, and the high architectonics which go with complete poetic development, are not required, he is perfect. Shakespearian work it is; not imitative, indeed, of Shakespeare, but Shakespearian, because its expression has that rounded perfection and felicity of loveliness of which Shakespeare is the great master. To show such work is to praise it. Let us now end by delighting ourselves with a fragment of it, far too beautiful to be lost. It is a fragment of an ode for
20 May Day. O might I, he cries to May, O might I

> . . . thy smiles
> Seek as they once were sought, in Grecian isles,
> By bards who died content on pleasant sward,
> Leaving great verse unto a little clan!
> O, give me their old vigour, and unheard
> Save of the quiet primrose, and the span
> Of heaven, and few years,
> Rounded by thee, my song should die away,
> Content as theirs,
> 30 Rich in the simple worship of a day!

NEWMAN

1884. *Discourses in America* (1885)

FORTY years ago, when I was an undergraduate at Oxford, voices were in the air there which haunt my memory still.

Happy the man who in that susceptible season of youth
hears such voices! they are a possession to him for ever. No
such voices as those which we heard in our youth at Oxford
are sounding there now. Oxford has more criticism now,
more knowledge, more light; but such voices as those of our
youth it has no longer. The name of Cardinal Newman is a
great name to the imagination still; his genius and his style
are still things of power. But he is over eighty years old; he
is in the Oratory at Birmingham; he has adopted, for the
doubts and difficulties which beset men's minds to-day, a 10
solution which, to speak frankly, is impossible. Forty years
ago he was in the very prime of life; he was close at hand
to us at Oxford; he was preaching in St. Mary's pulpit every
Sunday; he seemed about to transform and to renew what
was for us the most national and natural institution in the
world, the Church of England. Who could resist the charm
of that spiritual apparition, gliding in the dim afternoon
light through the aisles of St. Mary's, rising into the pulpit,
and then, in the most entrancing of voices, breaking the
silence with words and thoughts which were a religious 20
music,—subtle, sweet, mournful? I seem to hear him still,
saying: 'After the fever of life, after wearinesses and sick-
nesses, fightings and despondings, languor and fretfulness,
struggling and succeeding; after all the changes and chances
of this troubled, unhealthy state,—at length comes death,
at length the white throne of God, at length the beatific
vision.' Or, if we followed him back to his seclusion at
Littlemore, that dreary village by the London road, and to
the house of retreat and the church which he built there,—
a mean house such as Paul might have lived in when he was 30
tent-making at Ephesus, a church plain and thinly sown
with worshippers,—who could resist him there either, wel-
coming back to the severe joys of church-fellowship, and of
daily worship and prayer, the firstlings of a generation which
had well-nigh forgotten them?

CLOUGH

1861. Last Words on Translating Homer (1862)

How can I help remembering what a mind and character we have lost in losing Mr. Clough, whose name has more than once occurred in my lectures on Homer? He, too, was busy with Homer; but it is not on that account that I now speak of him. Nor do I speak of him in order to call attention to his qualities and powers in general, admirable as these were. I mention him because, in so eminent a degree, he possessed these two invaluable literary qualities: a true sense for his object of study, and a single-hearted care for it.
10 He had both; but he had the second even more eminently than the first. He greatly developed the first through means of the second. In the study of art, poetry, or philosophy, he had the most undivided and disinterested love for his object in itself, the greatest aversion to mixing up with it anything accidental or personal. His interest was in literature itself; and it was this which gave so rare a stamp to his character, which kept him so free from all taint of littleness. In the saturnalia of ignoble personal passions, of which the struggle for literary success, in old and crowded communities, offers
20 so sad a spectacle, he never mingled. He had not yet traduced his friends, nor flattered his enemies, nor disparaged what he admired, nor praised what he despised. Those who knew him well had the conviction that, even with time, these literary arts would never be his. His poem, 'The Bothie of Toper-na-Fuosich,' has some admirable Homeric qualities:—out-of-doors freshness, life, naturalness, buoyant rapidity. Some of the expressions in that poem,—'*Dangerous Corrievreckan. . . . Where roads are unknown to Loch Nevish,*'—come back now to my ear with
30 the true Homeric ring. But that in him of which I think oftenest, is the Homeric simplicity of his literary life.

ARMINIUS AND THE J.P.s

1867. *Friendship's Garland* (1871)

WE were going out the other morning on one of our walks, when we saw a crowd before the inn of the country town where we have been staying. It was the magistrates' day for sitting, and I was glad of an opportunity to show off our local self-government to a bureaucracy-ridden Prussian like Arminius. So I stopped in the crowd, and there we saw an old fellow in a smock-frock, with a white head, a low forehead, a red nose, and a foxy expression of countenance, being taken along to the justice-room. Seeing among the bystanders a contributor to the *Daily Telegraph*,[1] whom I 10 formerly knew well enough,—for he had the drawing-room floor underneath me in Grub Street, but the magnificent circulation of that journal has long since carried him, like the course of empire, westward,—I asked him if he could tell me what the prisoner was charged with. I found it was a hardened old poacher, called Diggs,—Zephaniah Diggs,— and that he was had up for snaring a hare,—probably his ten-thousandth. The worst of the story, to my mind, was that the old rogue had a heap of young children by a second wife whom he had married late in life, and that not one of 20 these children would he send to school, but persisted in letting them all run wild, and grow up in utter barbarism.

I hastened to tell Arminius that it was a poaching case; and I added that it was not always, perhaps, in poaching cases that our local self-government appeared to the best advantage. 'In the present case, however, there is,' said I, 'no danger; for a representative of the *Daily Telegraph* is down here, to be on the look-out for justices' justice, and to

[1] Do you recognise yourself, Leo? Is it presumptuous in me, upon giving this volume to the world, to bid you too, my friend, say with the poet: *Non omnis moriar?*—ED.

prevent oppression.' Immediately afterwards I was sorry I
had said this, for there are unfortunately several things
which operate on Arminius like scarlet on a bull, making
him vicious the moment he comes across them; and the
Daily Telegraph is one of these things. He declares it
foments our worst faults; and he is fond of applying to it
Dryden's dictum on Elkanah Settle, that its style is boisterous and its prose incorrigibly lewd. Though I do certainly
think its prose a little full-bodied, yet I cannot bear to hear
10 Arminius apply such a term to it as 'incorrigibly lewd;' and
I always remonstrate with him. 'No, Arminius,' I always
say, 'I hope not *incorrigibly*; I should be sorry to think that
of a publication which is forming the imagination and taste
of millions of Englishmen.' 'Pleasant news,' was Arminius's
answer, the last time I urged this to him, 'pleasant news;
the next batch of you, then, will be even more charming
than the present!'

I trouble you with all this, Sir, to account for the acerbity
of tone in some of Arminius's subsequent conversation; an
20 acerbity he too often manifests, and which tends, as I tell
him, to detract from the influence which his talents and
acquirements would otherwise give him. On the present
occasion he took no direct notice of my mention of the *Daily
Telegraph*, but seemed quite taken up with scrutinising old
Diggs. 'Such a peasant as that wretched old creature,' he
said at last, 'is peculiar, my dear friend, to your country.
Only look at that countenance! Centuries of feudalism have
effaced in it every gleam of humane life.' . . 'Centuries of
fiddlesticks!' interrupted I (for I assure you, Sir, I can stand
30 up to Arminius well enough on a proper occasion). 'My dear
Arminius, how can you allow yourself to talk such rubbish?
Gleam of humane life, indeed! do but look at the twinkle in
the old rogue's eye. He has plenty of life and wits about
him, has old Diggs, I can assure you; you just try and come
round him about a pot of beer!' 'The mere cunning of an

animal!' retorted Arminius. 'For my part,' pursued I, 'it
is his children I think most about; I am told not one of them
has ever seen the inside of a school. Do you know, Arminius,
I begin to think, and many people in this country begin to
think, that the time has almost come for taking a leaf out
of your Prussian book, and applying, in the education of
children of this class, what the great Kant calls the categorical imperative. The gap between them and our educated
and intelligent classes is really too frightful.' 'Your educated and intelligent classes!' sneered Arminius, in his very 10
most offensive manner; 'where are they? I should like to
see them.'

I was not going to stand and hear our aristocracy and
middle-class set down in this way; so, treating Arminius's
ebullition of spite as beneath my notice, I pushed my way
through the crowd to the inn-door. I asked the policeman
there what magistrates were on the bench to-day. 'Viscount
Lumpington,' says the man, 'Reverend Esau Hittall, and
Bottles Esquire.' 'Good heavens!' I exclaimed, turning
round to Arminius, who had followed me, and forgetting, 20
in my excitement, my just cause of offence with him,—
'Good heavens, Arminius, if Bottles hasn't got himself made
a county magistrate! *Sic itur ad astra.*' 'Yes,' says Arminius, with a smile, 'one of your educated and intelligent
classes, I suppose. And I dare say the other two are to
match. Your magistrates are a sort of judges, I know; just
the people who are drawn from the educated and intelligent
classes. Now, what's sauce for the goose is sauce for the
gander; if you put a pressure on one class to make it train
itself properly, you must put a pressure on others to the 30
same end. That is what we do in Prussia, if you are going
to take a leaf out of our book. I want to hear what steps
you take to put this pressure on people above old Diggs
there, and then I will talk to you about putting it on old
Diggs. Take his judges who are going to try him to-day;

how about them? What training have you made them give
themselves, and what are their qualifications?

I luckily happen to know Lord Lumpington and Hittall
pretty well, having been at college with them in former days,
when I little thought the Philistines would have brought my
grey hairs to a garret in Grub Street; and I have made the
acquaintance of Mr. Bottles since, and know all about him.
So I was able to satisfy Arminius's curiosity, and I had great
pleasure in making him remark, as I did so, the rich diversity
10 of our English life, the healthy natural play of our free
institutions, and the happy blending of classes and characters which this promotes. 'The three magistrates in that
inn,' said I, 'are not three Government functionaries all cut
out of one block; they embody our whole national life;—
the land, religion, commerce, are all represented by them.
Lord Lumpington is a peer of old family and great estate;
Esau Hittall is a clergyman; Mr. Bottles is one of our self-
made middle-class men. Their politics are not all of one
colour, and that colour the Government's. Lumpington is
20 a Constitutional Whig; Hittall is a benighted old Tory. As
for Mr. Bottles, he is a Radical of the purest water; quite
one of the Manchester school. He was one of the earliest
free-traders; he has always gone as straight as an arrow
about Reform; he is an ardent voluntary in every possible
line, opposed the Ten Hours' Bill, was one of the leaders of
the Dissenting opposition out of Parliament which smashed
up the education clauses of Sir James Graham's Factory
Act; and he paid the whole expenses of a most important
church-rate contest out of his own pocket. And, finally, he
30 looks forward to marrying his deceased wife's sister. Table
the whole Liberal creed, and in not a single point of it will
you find Bottles tripping!'

'That is all very well as to their politics,' said Arminius,
'but I want to hear about their education and intelligence.'
'There, too, I can satisfy you,' I answered. 'Lumpington

was at Eton. Hittall was on the foundation at Charterhouse,
placed there by his uncle, a distinguished prelate, who was
one of the trustees. You know we English have no notion
of your bureaucratic tyranny of treating the appointments
to these great foundations as public patronage, and vesting
them in a responsible minister; we vest them in independent
magnates, who relieve the State of all work and responsibi-
lity, and never take a shilling of salary for their trouble.
Hittall was the last of six nephews nominated to the Charterhouse by his uncle, this good prelate, who had thoroughly 10
learnt the divine lesson that charity begins at home.' 'But
I want to know what his nephew learnt,' interrupted Arminius, 'and what Lord Lumpington learnt at Eton.' 'They
followed,' said I, 'the grand, old, fortifying, classical curriculum.' 'Did they know anything when they left?' asked
Arminius. 'I have seen some longs and shorts of Hittall's,'
said I, 'about the Calydonian Boar, which were not bad.
But you surely don't need me to tell you, Arminius, that it
is rather in training and bracing the mind for future acquisi-
tion,—a course of mental gymnastics we call it,—than in 20
teaching any set thing, that the classical curriculum is so
valuable.' 'Were the minds of Lord Lumpington and Mr.
Hittall much braced by their mental gymnastics?' inquired
Arminius. 'Well,' I answered, 'during their three years at
Oxford they were so much occupied with Bullingdon and
hunting that there was no great opportunity to judge. But
for my part I have always thought that their both getting
their degree at last with flying colours, after three weeks of
a famous coach for fast men, four nights without going to
bed, and an incredible consumption of wet towels, strong 30
cigars, and brandy-and-water, was one of the most astonish-
ing feats of mental gymnastics I ever heard of.'

'That will do for the land and the Church,' said Arminius.
'And now let us hear about commerce.' 'You mean how
was Bottles educated?' answered I. 'Here we get into

another line altogether, but a very good line in its way, too. Mr. Bottles was brought up at the Lycurgus House Academy, Peckham. You are not to suppose from the name of Lycurgus that any Latin and Greek was taught in the establishment; the name only indicates the moral discipline, and the strenuous earnest character, imparted there. As to the instruction, the thoughtful educator who was principal of the Lycurgus House Academy,—Archimedes Silverpump, Ph.D., you must have heard of him in Germany?—had
10 modern views. "We must be men of our age," he used to say. "Useful knowledge, living languages, and the forming of the mind through observation and experiment, these are the fundamental articles of my educational creed." Or, as I have heard his pupil Bottles put it in his expansive moments after dinner (Bottles used to ask me to dinner till that affair of yours with him in the Reigate train): "Original man, Silverpump! fine mind! fine system! None of your antiquated rubbish—all practical work—latest discoveries in science— mind constantly kept excited—lots of interesting experi-
20 ments—lights of all colours—fizz! fizz! bang! bang!. That's what I call forming a man."'

'And pray,' cried Arminius, impatiently, 'what sort of man do you suppose this infernal quack really formed in your precious friend Mr. Bottles?' 'Well,' I replied, 'I hardly know how to answer that question. Bottles has certainly made an immense fortune; but as to Silverpump's effect on his mind, whether it was from any fault in the Lycurgus House system, whether it was that with a sturdy self-reliance thoroughly English, Bottles, ever since he
30 quitted Silverpump, left his mind wholly to itself, his daily newspaper, and the Particular Baptist minister under whom he sate, or from whatever cause it was, certainly his mind, *quâ* mind——' 'You need not go on,' interrupted Arminius, with a magnificent wave of his hand, 'I know what that man's mind, *quâ* mind, is, well enough.' . . .

'But,' continued Arminius, 'you were talking of compulsory education, and your common people's want of it.
Now, my dear friend, I want you to understand what this
principle of compulsory education really means. It means
that to ensure, as far as you can, every man's being fit for
his business in life, you put education as a bar, or condition,
between him and what he aims at. The principle is just as
good for one class as another, and it is only by applying it
impartially that you save its application from being insolent
and invidious. Our Prussian peasant stands our compelling
him to instruct himself before he may go about his calling,
because he sees we believe in instruction, and compel our
own class, too, in a way to make it really feel the pressure,
to instruct itself before it may go about its calling. Now,
you propose to make old Diggs's boys instruct themselves
before they may go bird-scaring or sheep-tending. I want
to know what you do to make those three worthies in that
justice-room instruct themselves before they may go acting
as magistrates and judges.' 'Do?' said I; 'why, just look
what they have done all of themselves. Lumpington and
Hittall have had a public-school and university education;
Bottles has had Dr. Silverpump's, and the practical training
of business. What on earth would you have us make them
do more?' 'Qualify themselves for administrative or judi-
cial functions, if they exercise them,' said Arminius. 'That
is what really answers, in their case, to the compulsion you
propose to apply to Diggs's boys. Sending Lord Lumpington and Mr. Hittall to school is nothing; the natural course
of things takes them there. Don't suppose that, by doing
this, you are applying the principle of compulsory education
fairly, and as you apply it to Diggs's boys. You are not
interposing, for the rich, education as a bar or condition
between them and that which they aim at. But interpose
it, as we do, between the rich and things they aim at, and
I will say something to you. I should like to know what has

made Lord Lumpington a magistrate?' 'Made Lord Lumpington a magistrate?' said I; 'why, the Lumpington estate,
to be sure.' 'And the Reverend Esau Hittall?' continued
Arminius. 'Why, the Lumpington living, of course,' said I.
'And that man Bottles?' he went on. 'His English energy
and self-reliance,' I answered very stiffly, for Arminius's
incessant carping began to put me in a huff; 'those same
incomparable and truly British qualities which have just
triumphed over every obstacle and given us the Atlantic
10 telegraph!—and let me tell you, Von T., in my opinion it
will be a long time before the "Geist" of any pedant of a
Prussian professor gives us anything half so valuable as
that.' 'Pshaw!' replied Arminius, contemptuously; 'that
great rope, with a Philistine at each end of it talking
inutilities!

'But in my country,' he went on, 'we should have begun
to put a pressure on these future magistrates at school.
Before we allowed Lord Lumpington and Mr. Hittall to go
to the university at all, we should have examined them, and
20 we should not have trusted the keepers of that absurd
cockpit you took me down to see, to examine them as they
chose, and send them jogging comfortably off to the university on their lame longs and shorts. No; there would have
been some Mr. Grote as School Board Commissary, pitching
into them questions about history, and some Mr. Lowe, as
Crown Patronage Commissary, pitching into them questions
about English literature; and these young men would have
been kept from the university, as Diggs's boys are kept from
their bird-scaring, till they had instructed themselves. Then,
30 if, after three years of their university, they wanted to be
magistrates, another pressure!—a great Civil Service examination before a board of experts, an examination in English
law, Roman law, English history, history of jurisprudence
——' 'A most abominable liberty to take with Lumpington
and Hittall!' exclaimed I. 'Then your compulsory educa-

tion is a most abominable liberty to take with Diggs's boys,'
retorted Arminius. 'But, good gracious! my dear Arminius,'
expostulated I, 'do you really mean to maintain that a man
can't put old Diggs in quod for snaring a hare without all
this elaborate apparatus of Roman law and history of jurisprudence?' 'And do you really mean to maintain,' returned
Arminius, 'that a man can't go bird-scaring or sheep-tending
without all this elaborate apparatus of a compulsory school?'
'Oh, but,' I answered, 'to live at all, even at the lowest stage
of human life, a man needs instruction.' 'Well,' returned 10
Arminius, 'and to administer at all, even at the lowest stage
of public administration, a man needs instruction.' 'We
have never found it so,' said I.

LITERATURE AND SCIENCE

1882. *Discourses in America* (1885)

PROFESSOR Huxley holds up to scorn mediæval education,
with its neglect of the knowledge of nature, its poverty even
of literary studies, its formal logic devoted to 'showing how
and why that which the Church said was true must be true.'
But the great mediæval Universities were not brought into
being, we may be sure, by the zeal for giving a jejune and
contemptible education. Kings have been their nursing 20
fathers, and queens have been their nursing mothers, but
not for this. The mediæval Universities came into being,
because the supposed knowledge, delivered by Scripture and
the Church, so deeply engaged men's hearts, by so simply,
easily, and powerfully relating itself to their desire for conduct, their desire for beauty. All other knowledge was domi-
nated by this supposed knowledge and was subordinated to
it, because of the surpassing strength of the hold which it
gained upon the affections of men, by allying itself profoundly with their sense for conduct, their sense for beauty. 30
But now, says Professor Huxley, conceptions of the uni-

verse fatal to the notions held by our forefathers have been
forced upon us by physical science. Grant to him that they
are thus fatal, that the new conceptions must and will soon
become current everywhere, and that every one will finally
perceive them to be fatal to the beliefs of our forefathers.
The need of humane letters, as they are truly called, because
they serve the paramount desire in men that good should be
for ever present to them,—the need of humane letters, to
establish a relation between the new conceptions, and our
10 instinct for beauty, our instinct for conduct, is only the more
visible. The Middle Age could do without humane letters,
as it could do without the study of nature, because its supposed knowledge was made to engage its emotions so powerfully. Grant that the supposed knowledge disappears, its
power of being made to engage the emotions will of course
disappear along with it,—but the emotions themselves, and
their claim to be engaged and satisfied, will remain. Now if
we find by experience that humane letters have an undeniable power of engaging the emotions, the importance of
20 humane letters in a man's training becomes not less, but
greater, in proportion to the success of modern science in
extirpating what it calls 'mediæval thinking.'

Have humane letters, then, have poetry and eloquence,
the power here attributed to them of engaging the emotions,
and do they exercise it? And if they have it and exercise it,
how do they exercise it, so as to exert an influence upon man's
sense for conduct, his sense for beauty? Finally, even if they
both can and do exert an influence upon the senses in question, how are they to relate to them the results,—the mod-
30 ern results,—of natural science? All these questions may be
asked. First, have poetry and eloquence the power of calling
out the emotions? The appeal is to experience. Experience
shows that for the vast majority of men, for mankind in
general, they have the power. Next, do they exercise it?
They do. But then, *how* do they exercise it so as to affect

man's sense for conduct, his sense for beauty? And this is
perhaps a case for applying the Preacher's words: 'Though
a man labour to seek it out, yet he shall not find it; yea,
farther, though a wise man think to know it, yet shall he
not be able to find it.' Why should it be one thing, in its
effect upon the emotions, to say, 'Patience is a virtue,' and
quite another thing, in its effect upon the emotions, to say
with Homer,

$$\tau\lambda\eta\tau\grave{o}\nu \ \gamma\grave{a}\rho \ Mo\hat{\iota}\rho\alpha\iota \ \theta\upsilon\mu\grave{o}\nu \ \theta\acute{\epsilon}\sigma\alpha\nu \ \grave{a}\nu\theta\rho\acute{\omega}\pi o\iota\sigma\iota\nu—$$

'for an enduring heart have the destinies appointed to the
children of men'? Why should it be one thing, in its effect
upon the emotions, to say with the philosopher Spinoza,
Felicitas in eo consistit quod homo suum esse conservare potest
—'Man's happiness consists in his being able to preserve his
own essence,' and quite another thing, in its effect upon the
emotions, to say with the Gospel, 'What is a man advan-
taged, if he gain the whole world, and lose himself, forfeit
himself?' How does this difference of effect arise? I cannot
tell, and I am not much concerned to know; the important
thing is that it does arise, and that we can profit by it. But
how, finally, are poetry and eloquence to exercise the power
of relating the modern results of natural science to man's
instinct for conduct, his instinct for beauty? And here again
I answer that I do not know *how* they will exercise it, but
that they can and will exercise it I am sure. I do not mean
that modern philosophical poets and modern philosophical
moralists are to come and relate for us, in express terms, the
results of modern scientific research to our instinct for conduct, our instinct for beauty. But I mean that we shall find,
as a matter of experience, if we know the best that has been
thought and uttered in the world, we shall find that the art
and poetry and eloquence of men who lived, perhaps, long
ago, who had the most limited natural knowledge, who had
the most erroneous conceptions about many important

matters, we shall find that this art, and poetry, and eloquence, have in fact not only the power of refreshing and delighting us, they have also the power,—such is the strength and worth, in essentials, of their authors' criticism of life,—they have a fortifying, and elevating, and quickening, and suggestive power, capable of wonderfully helping us to relate the results of modern science to our need for conduct, our need for beauty. Homer's conceptions of the physical universe were, I imagine, grotesque; but really,

10 under the shock of hearing from modern science that 'the world is not subordinated to man's use, and that man is not the cynosure of things terrestrial,' I could, for my own part, desire no better comfort than Homer's line which I quoted just now,

τλητὸν γὰρ Μοῖραι θυμὸν θέσαν ἀνθρώποισιν—

'for an enduring heart have the destinies appointed to the children of men'!

And the more that men's minds are cleared, the more that the results of science are frankly accepted, the more that

20 poetry and eloquence come to be received and studied as what in truth they really are,—the criticism of life by gifted men, alive and active with extraordinary power at an unusual number of points;—so much the more will the value of humane letters, and of art also, which is an utterance having a like kind of power with theirs, be felt and acknowledged, and their place in education be secured. . . .

I said that before I ended I would just touch on the question of classical education, and I will keep my word. Even if literature is to retain a large place in our education, yet

30 Latin and Greek, say the friends of progress, will certainly have to go. Greek is the grand offender in the eyes of these gentlemen. The attackers of the established course of study think that against Greek, at any rate, they have irresistible arguments. Literature may perhaps be needed in education,

they say; but why on earth should it be Greek literature? Why not French or German? Nay, has not an Englishman models in his own literature of every kind of excellence? As before, it is not on any weak pleadings of my own that I rely for convincing the gainsayers; it is on the constitution of human nature itself, and on the instinct of self-preservation in humanity. The instinct for beauty is set in human nature, as surely as the instinct for knowledge is set there, or the instinct for conduct. If the instinct for beauty is served by Greek literature and art as it is served by no other literature 10 and art, we may trust to the instinct of self-preservation in humanity for keeping Greek as part of our culture. We may trust to it for even making the study of Greek more prevalent than it is now. Greek will come, I hope, some day to be studied more rationally than at present; but it will be increasingly studied as men increasingly feel the need in them for beauty, and how powerfully Greek art and Greek literature can serve this need. . . .

And so we at last find, it seems, we find flowing in favour of the humanities the natural and necessary stream of things, 20 which seemed against them when we started. The 'hairy quadruped furnished with a tail and pointed ears, probably arboreal in his habits,' this good fellow carried hidden in his nature, apparently, something destined to develop into a necessity for humane letters. Nay, more; we seem finally to be even led to the further conclusion that our hairy ancestor carried in his nature, also, a necessity for Greek.

And therefore, to say the truth, I cannot really think that humane letters are in much actual danger of being thrust out from their leading place in education, in spite of the 30 array of authorities against them at this moment. So long as human nature is what it is, their attractions will remain irresistible. As with Greek, so with letters generally: they will some day come, we may hope, to be studied more rationally, but they will not lose their place. What will

happen will rather be that there will be crowded into education other matters besides, far too many; there will be,
perhaps, a period of unsettlement and confusion and false
tendency; but letters will not in the end lose their leading
place. If they lose it for a time, they will get it back again.
We shall be brought back to them by our wants and aspirations. And a poor humanist may possess his soul in patience,
neither strive nor cry, admit the energy and brilliancy of
the partisans of physical science, and their present favour
10 with the public, to be far greater than his own, and still have
a happy faith that the nature of things works silently on
behalf of the studies which he loves, and that, while we shall
all have to acquaint ourselves with the great results reached
by modern science, and to give ourselves as much training
in its disciplines as we can conveniently carry, yet the
majority of men will always require humane letters, and so
much the more, as they have the more and the greater
results of science to relate to the need in man for conduct,
and to the need in him for beauty.

NOTES

PAGE 2. TO A FRIEND. The writers referred to are Homer, Epictetus, and Sophocles. The 'Wide Prospect' is Europe. Vespasian's son was Domitian.

PAGE 3. THE FORSAKEN MERMAN. Arnold took the theme from *Agnes and the Merman* (R. C. A. Prior, *Ancient Danish Ballads*, iii. 332).

PAGE 7. RESIGNATION. Fausta is believed to have been Arnold's sister Jane (Mrs. H. Ward, *A Writer's Recollections*, 39). A note to the poem says that the walk described (ll. 40–85) was that from the Inn at Wythburn, near Lake Thirlmere in Cumberland, over the fells to Watendlath. The Inn was the Nag's Head. From Watendlath the party would reach the road along Derwentwater to Keswick, 'the noisy town', and thence might get to the sea at Maryport.

PAGE 16. ISOLATION. On Marguerite, v. *Introduction*.

PAGE 18. OBERMANN. Étienne Pivert de Sénancour (1770–1846), a pessimistic writer, whose reflections on the futility of active life much impressed Arnold in his earlier years. They took the form in his *Obermann* of letters by an imaginary recluse, in retreat near the Col de Jaman, above Montreux and Vevey at the eastern end of the Lake of Leman or Geneva. A later poem, *Obermann Once More*, not in this selection, reverts to Arnold's early theme.

l. 5. *abandoned baths*. The baths of Leuk. Arnold says that the poem was conceived, and partly composed, in the valley going down from the foot of the Commi Pass towards the Rhone.

PAGE 21, l. 89. Cf. Homer, *Iliad*, xxi. 106.

PAGE 24, l. 179. *Capital of Pleasure*. Paris.

PAGE 25. MEMORIAL VERSES. Wordsworth died on 23 April 1850, and was buried at Grasmere on 27 April, the date ascribed by Arnold to this poem. Byron had died in 1824 and Goethe in 1832.

PAGE 26, l. 29. Cf. Virgil, *Georgics*, ii. 490—

    felix qui potuit rerum cognoscere causas,
    atque metus omnis et inexorabile fatum
    subiecit pedibus strepitumque Acherontis avari.

PAGE 27, l. 72. The Rotha flows by Grasmere Church.

PAGE 27. CADMUS AND HARMONIA. *Empedocles on Etna* versifies the supposed musings of a fifth-century Sicilian philosopher, said to have committed suicide by throwing him-

self into the crater of Mt. Etna. The songs of a lute-player
Callicles, which include this and the following poem, give a
lyric relief.

PAGE 30. YOUTH AND CALM. This was, in 1852, the latter
part of *Lines Written by a Death-bed*. The earlier part became
in 1869 part of the second episode, not here given, of *Tristram
and Iseult*.

PAGE 31. ISEULT OF BRITTANY. Arnold's *Tristram and
Iseult* is mainly based on an account of a twelfth-century
French romance on a Celtic theme. But the final episode,
here alone given, is his own addition, and incorporates the
story of Merlin and Vivian from Sir Thomas Malory's *Morte
Darthur*.

l. 3. Tyntagel was the seat of King Mark of Cornwall, whose
wife, Iseult of Ireland, Tristram loved, before he knew Iseult
of Brittany.

PAGE 35, l. 143. Suetonius, *De Vita Caesarum*, i. 7, records
the tears of Julius Caesar at the exploits of Alexander the
Great, who conquered the 'Soudan' Darius of Persia.

PAGE 38. A SUMMER NIGHT. Probably ll. 11–25 refer to
some episode in Arnold's relations with Marguerite.

PAGE 40, l. 65. The 'pale master' is probably just Man.

PAGE 41. YOUTH OF NATURE. Wordsworth died at Rydal
Mount, near the lake of that name, divided from Grasmere by
Mt. Fairfield. At Grasmere are or were the cottage called 'The
Evening Star' and the sheepfold of his *Michael*. Egremont and
the Pillar rock, both in West Cumberland, are named in his
The Brothers. His *Ruth* recalls an early sojourn at Alfoxden in
the Quantock hills of Somerset.

PAGE 52. The fight between the Persian champion, Rustum,
the son of Zal, and his own illegitimate and unknown son
Sohrab is told of in the *Shah Namah* (Book of Kings) of the
Persian poet Ferdousi (10th cent. A.D.). Arnold took it from
Sir John Malcolm's *History of Persia* and a review by Sainte
Beuve of Jules Mohl's translation of Ferdousi. It is an
episode of war between Persia, now Iran, and a confederacy of
mixed Tartar, Mongol, Slav, and Turkish tribes stretching
from Turkistan on the north-east to the Caspian Sea and the
Don basin on the west. Persia is ruled by Kai Khosroo, who
may be Cyrus the Great (6th cent. B.C.), and in it are
Seistan, Khorassan, and Ader-baijan, where Sohrab's mother
Tahminah, not named in the poem, lives with her father, a
sub-king of the Koords. The river Helmund and Lake Zirrah
are in the east of Persia, which is bordered by Afghanistan.

The Elburz mountains, where Zal was reared by the fabulous griffin, divide Persia from the Caspian Sea. Near them is Casbin. Bokhara, Samarcand, and Kara-Kul are towns in Turkistan. Salore has not been identified. The chief river of Turkestan is the Oxus, now the Amu Daria or Jihun, which comes from the Pamir mountains in central Asia, and flows through Orgunje and Khiva, also called Chorasmia, into the Aral Sea. The geography can be more fully studied in an edition of the poem by W. J. Cunningham Pike (1916), but many of the names, like those of minor characters, have little function, except to give sonority to the verse. The similes take a wider range. Cabool (Kabul) is in Afghanistan, Pekin in China, the Hyphasis (Sutlej), and Hydaspes (Jhelun) in India. The ruins of Persepolis, an old capital of Persia in the supposed days of Jemshid (*c.* 1000–800 B.C.), are near Shiraz.

PAGE 55, l. 111. Cf. Homer, *Iliad*, ii. 459.

PAGE 76, ll. 853–6. Cf. Homer, *Iliad*, xvi. 855–7, on the death of Patroclus.

> ὣς ἄρα μιν εἰπόντα τέλος θανάτοιο κάλυψε·
> ψυχὴ δ' ἐκ ῥεθέων πταμένη ''Ἀϊδόσδε βεβήκει,
> ὃν πότμον γοόωσα, λιποῦσ' ἀδροτῆτα καὶ ἥβην.

PAGE 77. THE TOMB. This is the last episode only of *The Church of Brou*. In the earlier ones Philibert, Duke of Savoy, dies from an accident during a boar-hunt. Historically, it was in 1504, from drinking cold water while heated with the chase. His wife, Marguerite of Austria, builds the church and tomb as a memorial, and herself dies when it is ready. Notre Dame de Brou is not in the mountains, but in the plain, at Bourg-en-Bresse, north-east of Lyon.

PAGE 79. THE SCHOLAR GIPSY. Arnold found the story of the Scholar Gipsy in Joseph Glanvill's *Vanity of Dogmatizing* (1661). But it is the poet himself who localizes the wanderings on the high Berkshire ground which runs, within a northwards loop of the Thames, from Bagley Wood and the adjacent Thessaly, above South and North Hinksey, to Cumnor and its Hurst. Godstow Bridge, two miles north of Oxford, and the ferry of Bablock Hythe, below Cumnor, are on the Thames itself. Fyfield stands farther back, on the road between Cumnor and Faringdon. Wychwood Forest is some miles away, on the Oxfordshire side of the river, near Charlbury. The 'causeway' (l. 121) is between Oxford and South Hinksey. Christ Church is an Oxford college.

PAGE 85, l. 182. Arnold said in 1883 that he meant Goethe (C. H. Leonard in *Modern Language Notes*, xlvi. 119).

PAGE **86,** l. 208. Cf. Virgil, *Aeneid*, vi. 450, *sqq*.

PAGE **88,** l. 249. Arnold probably had in mind the theory that the early inhabitants of Britain were Iberians.

PAGE **88.** THE GRANDE CHARTREUSE. A Carthusian monastery, near the source of the Guiers Mort river, fourteen miles from Grenoble in France. Courrerie was an outlying house belonging to it.

PAGE **92,** l. 115. Achilles may stand for Newman, who on his return from Rome in 1833, and shortly before he left the Church of England, founded with Hurrell Froude the *Lyra Apostolica*, which bore the motto, paraphrased from *Iliad*, xviii. 125, 'They shall know the difference, now I am back.'

ll. 133, 139. Byron died at Missolonghi in what had been Aetolia. Shelley was drowned yachting in the Gulf of Spezzia.

PAGE **93,** l. 145. On Obermann, cf. note to p. 18.

PAGE **95.** RUGBY CHAPEL. A reminiscence of the poet's father, Thomas Arnold, and of his influence over the generation brought up under him at Rugby School. He had died on 12 June 1842.

PAGE **98,** l. 110. The host is probably Old Age, rather than Death.

PAGE **101.** THYRSIS is a monody on Arnold's Rugby and Oxford friend, Arthur Hugh Clough (cf. p. 166), who died, after a restless and rather dissatisfied life, at Florence on the Arno in 1861. The setting is that of *The Scholar Gipsy* (p. 79). The Tree does not come from Glanvill's book, but certainly had an actual existence at some spot on the high Berkshire ridge above South and North Hinksey, probably not far from Cumnor. The three weirs (l. 15) may be those of Pink Hill, Skinner's Bridge, and Northmoor on the Upper Thames. Ensham, or Eynsham (l. 109) is lower down, and still lower the river curved below Wytham hill to the locks (l. 122) of Godstow and Medley, the latter of which has now gone. Sandford (l. 109) is below Oxford. For the Fyfield tree (l. 106) cf. p. 82, l. 83. Arnold wrote (*Letters*, ed. Russell, i. 325) that the diction of the poem was modelled on Theocritus. The images were all from actual observation, but the cuckoo (l. 57) was heard on a wet June morning at Woodford in Epping Forest, where Arnold stayed with his wife in 1864.

Sir Michael Sadler has identified Sibylla (l. 4), with Sybella Curr, who once kept the Cross Keys Inn in South Hinksey, whence a footpath leads to Childsworth, or Chilswell, Farm (l. 11).

PAGE **109.** AUSTERITY OF POETRY. The poet was Jacopone da

Todi, a rich and gay young lawyer. After his wife's death in 1268, he gave away his property, became a Franciscan, and died in 1306.

PAGE **110.** DOVER BEACH. l. 15. Cf. Sophocles, *Antigone*, 583, where the curse upon a house is compared to a storm throwing up breakers on a beach.

PAGE **118.** A SPEECH AT ETON. l. 5. Epictetus (ed. Schenkl), p. 204.

PAGE **121,** l. 2. Goethe (Weimar ed.), I, vol. 42ii, p. 211.

l. 14. Christian von Bunsen was Prussian ambassador to England (1841–54).

PAGE **122,** l. 1. Goethe, *Faust*, i, l. 167.

l. 12. Thucydides, ii. 35–46.

l. 27. E. Curtius, *Hist. of Greece*, ii. 516.

PAGE **123,** l. 18. F. v. Hellwald, *The Russians in Central Asia* (1874).

PAGE **124,** l. 12. Aristotle, *Nicomachean Ethics*, ii. 7. 13.

l. 18. Plato, *Republic*, p. 563.

l. 32. *Ephesians*, v. 4.

PAGE **125,** l. 9. Pindar, *Pythian Ode*, iv. 102.

PAGE **126,** l. 24. Isocrates, *Panegyricus*, iv. 50.

PAGE **129,** l. 12. *Ecclesiastes*, xi. 6.

l. 27. Hales, *Of Private Judgment in Religion* (*Works*, iii. 150).

PAGE **130,** l. 20. *Ecclesiastes*, xi. 7–9.

PAGE **132,** ll. 25, 33. Curtius, ii. 573; iv. 116.

PAGE **133,** ll. 13, 26. Curtius, iii. 132, 282.

l. 20. The exact phrase is not traceable in Aeschylus; it may be a summary of *Eumenides*, 526 *sqq.*

l. 31. Horace, *Epist.* ii. 1. 156.

PAGE **134,** l. 7. *Proverbs*, v. 6.

PAGE **137,** l. 2. De Tocqueville, *Démocratie en Amérique*, i. 11.

l. 30. *Deuteronomy*, iv. 6, 8.

PAGE **138,** l. 6. Cf. p. 126.

PAGE **139.** ASELGEIA = Dissoluteness.

l. 3. Plato, *Republic*, pp. 424, 588; W. Paley, *Moral and Political Philosophy*, III. iii, ch. ii (paraphrased).

PHILISTINES. Arnold probably borrowed the term from Heine.

PAGE **140.** BARBARIANS. Cf. p. 150, l. 25, note.

PAGE **143,** l. 12. Montesquieu, *Discours sur les Motifs qui doivent nous encourager aux Sciences*, in *Œuvres* (1846), 579.

PAGE **144,** l. 3. Thomas Wilson, *Works* (1796), ii. 303.

l. 11. Swift, *Works* (ed. Temple Scott), i. 172.

l. 19. *criticism of life*; i.e. discrimination, the sorting out of what is best in life.

PAGE **145,** ll. 20, 24. Wordsworth, *Preface to Lyrical Ballads* (1800).

PAGE **148.** Shakespeare, *Winter's Tale*, iv. 4. 118; *Sonnet* xxxii; *Hamlet*, v. 2. 10; Wordsworth, *Solitary Reaper*; Keats, *Last Sonnet*; Aeschylus, *Choephoroi*, 305; *Prometheus Vinctus*, 90.

PAGE **149,** l. 23. The story of Gwydion and Math is in Lady C. Guest's *Mabinogion*.

PAGE **150,** l. 25. Arnold parodies Byron, *Childe Harold*, iv. 141.

PAGE **151,** l. 16. Goethe, *Epilog zu Schillers Glocke*.

PAGE **152,** ll. 4, 16. Dryden, *Critical Essays* (ed. W. P. Ker) ii. 257, 262.

l. 14. Lydgate, *Lyfe of Oure Ladye*.

l. 15. Johnson, *Preface to Dictionary*.

l. 22. Spenser, *Faerie Queene*, iv. 2. 32.

PAGE **153,** l. 8. Dante, *Paradiso*, iii. 85 ('In' should be '**E**').

l. 18. Aristotle, *Poetics*, ch. ix.

PAGE **153.** Arnold's criticism of Shakespeare here, from a particular angle, must be read with his other references to him (e.g. l. 23 above and pp. 148, 163, 164). In *Essays in Criticism* (1888), 96, he writes: 'Shakespeare frequently has lines and passages in a strain quite false, and which are entirely unworthy of him. But one can imagine his smiling if one could meet him in the Elysian Fields and tell him so; smiling and replying that he knew it perfectly well himself, and what did it matter?'

PAGE **154,** l. 19. J. E. Spingarn, *Goethe's Literary Essays*, 72.

PAGE **155,** l. 12. *Paradise Lost*, iii. 36; xii. 644.

l. 21. *Prelude*, iii. 17.

PAGE **156,** l. 12. *The Recluse* (*ad fin.*).

l. 31. Wordsworth, *A Poet's Epitaph*, 58.

PAGE **157,** l. 14. *Edinburgh Review* (Nov. 1814).

ll. 24, 26. *Macbeth*, iii. 2. 23; *Paradise Lost*, vii. 25.

PAGE **158,** ll. 4, 15. *The Recluse* (*ad fin.*); *Michael*, 466.

l. 23. Burns, *A Bard's Epitaph*.

PAGE **159,** l. 20. Joseph Joubert, author of *Pensées* (1842).

PAGE **160,** l. 24. Goethe, *Conversations with Eckermann* (tr. 1850), i. 198.

PAGES **162–4.** KEATS. The quotations in verse are from *Ode to a Grecian Urn*, 49; *Endymion*, i. 1; *Ode to May*, 5; those in prose from Keats's *Letters* (ed. M. B. Forman, i. 72, 250, 261, 262;

ii. 341, 510), except the bit about Kean, which is from a notice of his performance in *The Champion* (*Works*, ed. H. B. Forman, iii. 4).

PAGE **164.** J. H. Newman was Vicar of the University Church of St. Mary at Oxford from 1828 to 1843, and retired to Littlemore in 1842.

PAGE **166.** CLOUGH. Cf. p. 101, note.

l. 25. Toper-na-Fuosich. Altered later to Tober-na-Vuolich.

PAGE **167.** ARMINIUS. In *Friendship's Garland* are comments on English civilization in Arnold's lightest and wittiest vein, contributed mainly to the *Pall Mall Gazette* during 1866–70, and ascribed by him to an imaginary Arminius von Thunder-Ten-Tronck, whom he claimed as a descendant of the family whose adventures were the subject of Voltaire's *Candide* (1759). His name, says Arnold, was really Hermann, but Arminius seemed more 'in the grand style'. The book was dedicated to Adolescens Leo, one of the 'young lions' of the *Daily Telegraph*. Arnold himself claims to dwell in Grub Street, the traditional abode of penniless hack-writers since the days of the eighteenth-century *Grub-street Journal*, inspired by Pope.

PAGE **167,** note. Horace, *Odes*, iii. 30, 6.

> non omnis moriar; multaque pars mei
> vitabit Libitinam.

PAGE **168,** l. 7. It was really Settle's 'rhyme' that Dryden (*Works*, xv. 399) called 'lewd'.

PAGE **169,** l. 7. Kant used the term 'categorical imperative' for the unconditional validity of the moral judgement.

l. 23. Virgil, *Aeneid*, ix. 641.

PAGE **170,** ll. 25, 27. The Ten Hours Bill (1847) and Factory Bill (1843) were early attempts at legislation for social better-ment.

PAGE **171,** l. 16. *longs and shorts*. Classical verses in quantitative metres.

l. 25. *Bullingdon*. An Oxford club, frequented by rich undergraduates.

PAGE **174,** ll. 23–6. George Grote (1794–1871), author of *History of Greece*, Vice-Chancellor of London University; Robert Lowe (1811–92) M.P. for London University (1868).

PAGE **177,** ll. 2–16. *Ecclesiastes*, viii. 17; Homer, *Iliad*, xxiv. 49; Spinoza, *Ethica* IV, xviii; *St. Luke*, ix. 25.

PAGE **179.** LITERATURE AND SCIENCE, l. 21. Darwin, *Descent of Man*, ch. xxi.

PRINTED IN
GREAT BRITAIN
AT THE
UNIVERSITY PRESS
OXFORD
BY
CHARLES BATEY
PRINTER
TO THE
UNIVERSITY